NATIONAL MEDIA POLICY

About the Author

V. S. Gupta, presently Professor at the Haryana Agricultural University, was awarded the UNDP Fellowship for training in Europe and was selected for the Journalist Fellowship Award for working in the area of Environment and Development.

He has contributed a large number of papers in seminars, conferences and academic journals in India and abroad. Some of the publications edited by him include : *Media and Development (1994)* with M. R. Dua and *Rural Press — Problems and Prospects (1995)* with Rajeshwar Dyal. His book, *Third Revolution in Indian Perspective : Contemporary Issues and Themes in Communication (1995)* has been very well received in India and abroad.

Prof. Gupta is associated with publications, academic programmes in journalism and mass communication at the post-graduate level of several universities in the country. He represents the Asian Mass Communication Research and Information Centre (AMIC) Singapore, as its representative in India.

Rajeshwar Dyal, has an experience of 20 years in communication research, training, development of training material, interaction with national and international media organisations and activists. Presently, he is working as Media Advisor with Friedrich Ebert Foundation, which aims at democratisation and pluralism in media, organising media activities with media in the government and private sector, academia from various departments and other research institutions. He was with the Indian Institute of Mass Communication, New Delhi for 15 years prior to his joining the present assignment in 1992.

NATIONAL MEDIA POLICY

Edited by

V. S. GUPTA
Professor
Directorate of Publications
Haryana Agricultural University,
Hisar

RAJESHWAR DYAL
Media Advisor
Friedrich Ebert Stiftung
New Delhi

Published for

AMIC
FRIEDRICH EBERT STIFTUNG

by

CONCEPT PUBLISHING COMPANY, NEW DELHI

ISBN 81-7022-644-9

First Published 1996

Published and Printed by
Ashok Kumar Mittal
Concept Publishing Company
A/15-16, Commercial Block,
Mohan Garden,
NEW DELHI - 110 059 (India)
Phones: 5554042, 5504042

PREFACE

Over the years the debate on formulating a National Media Policy has been a constant pre-occupation with UNESCO, media academics and institutes, non-governmental organisations and with the Ministry of Information and Broadcasting of the Government of India.

The International Commission for the Study of Communication Problems in its Report (1982) recommended : Communication be no longer regarded merely as an incidental service and its development left to chance. Recognition of its potential warrants the formulation by all nations, and particularly developing countries, of comprehensive communication policies linked to overall social, cultural, economic and political goals. Such policies should be based on inter-ministerial and inter-disciplinary consultations with broad public participation.

The Working Group on Autonomy for Akashvani and Doordarshan said : If the broadcast media in India have grown haphazardly it is because their role, as that of the media generally, has not been perceived as part of a well defined national communications policy which embraces everything to do with articulation, including education and culture, and physical movement. In her book, *Broadcasting and the People*, Mehra Masani attributed lack of progress in organised broadcasting to the absence of communication policy 35 years after the start of organised broadcasting, radio listening is still very restricted in spite of the extension of the radio network.

The Government of India, over the past more than 25 years, has formed several committees to study various aspects of media policy : autonomy of electronic media, software production, distribution of air time, cable television, etc. The Consultative Committee attached to the Ministry of Information and Broadcasting in its meetings held in July 1993 also had National Media Policy as one of the agenda items for discussion. The Committee was of the view that a National Media Policy as formulated; although there were differing opinions regarding its form and contents. Subsequently, the Ministry circulated a Note on National Media Policy — A Discussion Paper and a Questionnaire to elicit opinion from a cross section of society, including media professionals, experts and he general public.

In one of the seminars organized in 1994 in New Delhi, the Principal Information Officer, Government of India, Mr. Narendra said that media experts should suggest the format of national media policy to the government. At present there is no national media policy as such. However, there are broad guidelines and codes instituted for guiding Doordarshan, Akashvani, etc. The Press Council generally has a role to play in the print media. The Advertising Council of India has its own code for the advertising profession but there is no mechanism to oversee the implementation of these codes.

AMIC has also been actively promoting debate on National Media Policy. The AMIC Secretary General, Mr. Vijaya Menon stated in his message on the occasion of the National Colloquium : This Colloquium in New Delhi provides a fitting finale to the series of FES sponsored seminars on National Communication Policy that AMIC India has organized in different parts of the country. AMIC feels privileged to have been able, over a period of almost a quarter century, to promote debate on media policy and to aid in the development of the region's media. AMIC's pioneering efforts were made possible by the support provided by the Government of Singapore and the Friedrich Ebert Stiftung (FES). The FES has been an exemplary donor agency, supportive but non-interfering. Nowhere has this been better demostrated than in India.

In the Foreword to a recently released book, *Public Policy, Analysis and Design*, the eminent Indian diplomat, economist and educational administrator, Prof. A. M. Khusro has said, "Policy need not be made by governments only, but in this country policy has been made almost wholly by governments. It may be because other segments, sector and socio economic agents in the country — the private industrial sector, the commercial sector and the social sector have been weak and are in the throes of a slow developmental process, they will acquire a degree of resilience and a policy making capability later. But to begin with they are weak. And therefore, it fell to the lot of Central and State Governments to make policies and programmes during the last 40 years... I have already stated that non-governmental organizations (NGOs) that could make policies are still weak, but that they are emerging slowly. There are NGOs like Policy Initiatives or Policy Alternatives, etc. and there are the associations of industry and trade. Many people in the private sector of industry and trade, the cooperative sector, the NGO sector, the social sector and the intellectual sector are beginning to think of many policy areas and it is certain that their role will increase with time."

Keeping in view the importance of the National Media Policy for the country, AMIC India with support from FES decided to organize a series of four seminars in the country during 1995 — Chandigarh, 5-6 May; Bhopal, 9-10 September; Bangalore, 26-27 September and Rourkela, 14-15 October, 1995 and as a finale to the series of these seminars, a National Colloquium, hosted by the Indian Institute of Mass Communication in New Delhi on 9-10 November 1995. These seminars and the National Colloquium provided a suitable opportunity to the participants, AMIC members, Media Practitioners to deliberate on various aspects of the National Media Policy. The papers presented at these Seminars and the National Colloquium touched upon different aspects of the National Media Policy. The participants brought their varied and rich experience to bear upon the discussion on some of the critical issues through these papers. Some of these papers, alongwith a number of Annexures, have been put together in this publication for wider dissemination and to be of use for reference and consultation by the students and teachers of journalism, media practitioners and by other interested in National Media Policy. It has not been possible to take all the papers presented at these Seminars : only some of the selected ones have been used in this publication for wider public discussion and dissemination.

By way of elucidation, we may point out that in the present publication, several terms have been used — Communication, Communications, Media Policy/Policies, and Communication Policy/ Policies. In this context, the International Commission for the Study of Communication Problems (1982) clarified : Definitions of several general notions dealt with in this Report — more particularly, those of communication and information — have not been standardized nor is there a unanimity as to their meanings. In fact, the terms are used by different authors in a variety of ways, with many nuances regarding their components and significance.

The Discussion Paper on National Media Policy prepared by the Ministry of Information and Broadcasting has also stated that the present policy has been variously termed by both the government and those demanding it at various points of time as a Media Policy, an Information Policy and as a Communication Policy. Needless to say, all these convey possibly different meanings.

In the absence of any standardisation, we have, therefore, retained these terms in the context of the relevant texts or as indicated by the authors of various papers.

We take this opportunity of expressing our deep gratitude to all the participants, observers, chairmen and rapporteurs of various sessions and authorities of the host institutions who had collaborated in holding these seminars. We would particularly like to place on record our deep gratitude to Mr. P. A. Sangma, Union Minister for Information and Broadcasting; Mr. P. Upendra, Former Minister for Information and Broadcasting; Mr. P. Murari and Dr. J. S. Yadav — Chairman and Director, Indian Institute of Mass Communication, respectively; Mr. Ajit Bhattacharjea, Director, Press Institute of India; Mr. Kiran Karnik from Discovery Channel and Mr. P. V. Narayanamoorthy, Senior Vice-President (Media Services), MacCann Ericson.

We also feel deeply obliged to Dr. Peter Hering, Deputy Secretary General, AMIC, Shri Arvind Chaturvedi, Director-General, Makhanlal Chaturvedi National University of Journalism, Bhopal; eminent media educators — Dr. K. E. Eapen; Prof. M. R. Dua; Dr. B. S. Thakur; Prof. Abdur Rahim; Mr. Prem Kumar and other veteran academics and practitioners, who participated and guided the deliberations at various places. We received valuable support and guidance from the AMIC Secretary General, Mr. Vijay Menon and the Resident Representative-FES, Dr. Heinz Bongartz for which we place on record our deep gratitude. We also acknowledge the valuable support extended by our colleagues in AMIC—Mr R. V. Rajan, Mr. Ashok Panda and Mr. Ashish Sen.

We hope that the papers presented at these seminars and the proceedings of the Colloquium, which we have included in this book will go a long way in encouraging the debate and discussion on the National Media Policy in the country.

We also place on record our gratitude to FES for sponsoring these seminars and National Colloquium and also for the support for bringing out this publication.

V. S. Gupta
Country Representative, AMIC

Rajeshwar Dyal
Media Advisor, FES

CONTENTS

1

NATIONAL COMMUNICATION POLICIES

M. R. Dua

It is hard to define communication policies in universally acceptable terms. According to the International Commission for the Study of Communication Problems, popularly known as the Sean MacBride Commission, "There is little unanimity concerning the importance and necessity" on communication policies. This is so, as the commission points out, because the various global communication systems are "increasingly complex; because new technological advances require more planning and oversight; because the expansion of international communication has to be supported by internal measures".

According to the MacBride Commission, the communication policies "do not necessarily imply rigid, centralized planning, but may simply constitute a favourable framework for the coordination of activities, allowing flexibility and a wide choice of approaches to communication" strategies.

It has, however, been pointed out that the formulation of communication policies should (a) serve to marshal national resources; (b) strengthen the coordination of existing or planned infrastructures; (c) facilitate national choices with regard to means; (d) help to satisfy the needs of the most disadvantaged and to eliminate the most flagrant imbalances; (e) emphasize universal and continuing education; (f) help in strengthening cultural identity and national independence; (g) enable all countries and all cultures to play a more prominent role on international scene.

The need for formulating national communication policies has of late been increasingly felt, as astoundingly phenomenal strides have taken place in national and international communication and media scenario, most nations are puzzled, shocked and bewildered. For, increasingly international media are questioning, interpellating and probing into the ways and means of dealing with these mind-boggling developments. However, not many have so far been able to adequately or satisfactorily cope with daily new and extraordinary media advances. What is direly lacking is a regular scientifically structured realistic national communication media policy.

In India, the need for a national media policy has been under a prolonged debate. Most committees, sub-committees and commissions have invariably emphasized the need for a national media policy. A large number of critics, media professionals, researchers, sociologists, besides politicians and bureaucrats, have occasionally underlined the need for a properly formulated national communication media policy for the country.

As someone said at a national seminar pointed out that India has national policies for cement, fertilizer, sugar, newsprint, power, women, education, food and what have you, therefore, why not policy for the media? Yes, why not?

It was perhaps because of this overt reason that the Information and Broadcasting Ministry recently prepared and circulated a 64-page questionnaire on media policy. This elaborate document seeks the views on national media policy of media professionals, critics and from all those who wish to respond to the questionnaire.

The document contains general questions on print media, including news agencies, small and medium, and language newspapers, foreign press, social responsibilities of the press; readers and rights; standards of journalism; government and the press; electronic media, radio, television, including film media and films division; central board of film certification; film festivals; film cultural exchange weeks; selection of Indian panorama film, international film festival of India, national film development corporation, national film archives of India, and film and television institute of India.

The question of determining and adopting a media policy has been dogging the authorities for a long time now. Several media committees in the past such as those headed by Asok Chanda, B. G. Verghese, P. C. Joshi, particularly the commissions headed by Kuldip Nayar, Justices K. K. Mathew, P. K. Goswamy and G. S. Rajadhyaksha have tried to grapple with the issue. However, the question on the universally accepted media policy has defied solution so far. The government has, therefore, taken a wise step in soliciting the opinions of all those who have been craving for an answer all these years.

The fact of the matter is that though just as communication is part and parcel of human existence and so very vital for an individual's survival, communication policy is a fundamental requisite for a country's image and PR effort. A nation without a meticulously framed national communication programme is like a computer without a floppy, or a typewriter without a ribbon.

In this first instance, it will be appropriate here to spell out as to what we mean by a national communication media policy. According to a UNESCO document, communication policies are "sets of principles and norms established to guide the behaviour of communication systems". Another view is that "communication policies are laws, rules, regulations and traditions in the field of mass communication... rules and regulations that govern the operation of newspapers, radio, television, video and films."

It is these rules and regulations that determine government media relationship and public access to media and telecommunication services. These factors are extremely significant for enabling masses to avail themselves fully of media services of their choice and preference. In fact, the absence of such options will mean regimentation and denial of basic human rights.

Generally speaking, the objectives of national communication policies are to inform masses about the developments taking place in national and international spheres affecting their daily life. These policies also help inspire, motivate and enthuse the people to support and cooperate in nation-building, economic progress, social development, imbibe national cultural values and education. Communication policies also assist coordination and cooperation among multifarious national and international agencies; promote rational thinking and deal with national problems in a logical, systematic manner. The most crucial objective, however, is to bring about overall wider acceptance of programmes for national development keeping the fast changing global communication scenario.

The state of the national communication policies in India is indeed intriguing. The freedom of the press is guaranteed under Article 19(i) (a) of the Constitution. While the print media, particularly, the daily press, are under the private sector control and operate as individual enterprises like other private industrial units, national electronic media are under direct control of the union government through information and broadcasting ministry.

In addition, whereas the private daily and periodical press is basically profit-motivated, and generally abide by journalistic norms, standards and social responsibilities, for the state-owned electronic media, perpetuation and dissemination of the national government's policies and programmes are the prime functions. As an I&B ministry's recent publication, the "Doordarshan, 1995", says : The social objectives of Doordarshan are to : act as a catalyst for social changes; promote national integration; stimulate a scientific temper; disseminate the family planning message; agriculture; environment; highlight the need for social welfare measures; inculcate interest in sports; and create values of artistic and cultural heritage.

Almost identical are the objects of All India Radio, besides of course that AIR "will broadcast programmes to listeners all over the country... and that these programmes will include a good deal of entertainment, and an appropriate amount of informative and educative programmes and also news and discussions on topical matters in suitable measures." The I&B ministry at the centre, by and large, frames policies for its media units, these are the communication policies which in a way can commulatively be deemed to be the nation's communication policies.

Thus, the I&B ministry's 1995 Annual Report says : "The I&B ministry provides comprehensive information on the policies, plans and projects of the government of India..." Its media units seek to create a climate of awareness of the directions of development and ensure people's participation in implementation of government's plans and programmes".

Mass media in India, electronic and print, are today truly at crossroads. While the language press day in and day out has been trying to present a wholly new panoramic view of the nation's development in diverse areas such as social, rural, economic, political, cultural and educational, the English language print media have been extensively adopting elitist, urban and western outlook. Though foreign papers have not yet arrived in India, but those in Paris, London, New York, Los Angeles, Washington and Bonn have entered into some kind of arrangements by which their stories are reproduced in Indian newspapers day in and day out for us to read. The result is that our young generation in the metros may not know what is happening in the far flung areas of Itanagar or Itarsi, Kittur, Kutch or Katra, but they can reel out the minutest details about Madonna, Hugh Grant or Elvis. Newspaper and magazine features lifted from New York Times, Washington Post, London's, The Times, and The Telegraph, fill the bill. So what kind of print media policy can we frame to meet or curb these fastly emerging trends and needs?

Again, in India today the electronic media are totally in agonizingly thrilling-cum--abnoxious state. As terrestial and cable channels multiply, viewer's curiosities and anxieties also leapfrog. Many homes present the scenes of "civil war" between parents and the younger members of the family. As the prime time nears in the evenings, the elderly wish to watch the World News, Parkh or Eyewitness, young folk wait with bated breath to discover the next moves in popular serials as so many satellite channels offer every evening. Thus, what kind of national media policy or national communication programmes are these which offer titillating, enticing, alluring views to our citizens of the future? Can we stop this, change this or re-format this kind of electronic media fare?

The answer is a big no. For, one thing, modern communication technology has broken all the barriers. And once having allowed STAR, CNN, ZEE, BBC and all of their ilk, we cannot backtrack. One of the most prominent pillars of our democratic functioning is freedom to impart and receive information. The disastrous consequences of denial of this right in the former Soviet Union and eastern Europe are before us. Therefore, censorship or banning of satellite or cable is out of the question. The newly framed media policies have, therefore, to take cognizance of these existing realities.

There is yet another side of the story : while those living in the urban areas have 24-hour facility of electric supply, most parts of the countryside receive power for a couple of hours only. The people in villages don't get to watch even Krishi Darshan and news bulletins. Moreover, more than 70 per cent of our population in villages has yet to get cable or satellite connexions. So, they will not be affected by such TV fare which worries us, the urbanites.

But, there is still another paradox in our present situation : it is those people who live in big cities and towns who ultimately form the ruling class; they are the future decisions makers, policy-framers, nation's planners and architects in the literal sense. And they have during all their formative years, watched, lived and grown up with ZEE, STAR, CNN, ATN... When they reach such crucial stage of deciding the fortunes of the masses, what kind of visions of communication planning will they have? It can be easily imagined than explained.

So, therefore, what sort of communication media policy are we talking about? And, for whom? What are, therefore, the alternatives in such a dicey predicament? While on the one side, the old moral order loses its shine, and with pulls and pressures, on the other side, the modern economic systems offer radical transformation and dynamic revolution in ameliorating our deteriorating and impoverishing millions. But there are several side ill effects. The choice indeed is hard, difficult and limited.

To satisfactorily compete and meet the aspiration of diverse audiences is difficult indeed. As Doordarshan software committee's former chairman

P. C. Joshi once said : "The truth is that in a large and diverse country, the communication system must function as a responsive and responsible system, giving scope to all sections of the people to articulate their concern and needs, and to creative persons to contribute towards shaping policy and making programmes."

One asks : shaping policy and making programmes for whom? For, if you prepare programmes for the 70 per cent in rural areas, will they be facilitated to watch these; because, electricity is not there to set the "idiot box" aglow. Besides, the programmes that suit, interest or concern the 70 per cent rural people, will these also attract the rest 30 per cent, the "creamy layer" of the national audience? Since the sociological, economic, educational, political and cultural differences in both sets of audience are so sharp and glaring, no amount of policy, artistic skill or communication expertise can help devise and produce programmes which can prove equally absorbing for all sorts of audiences at the same time.

This, therefore, indeed is a prodigious dilemma for the electronic media. The situation at present is that of the 70 per cent rural audience, some 14 per cent own television sets and tune in mostly in the evening when electric current is available to watch news or entertainment, film or film-based programmes. This has been brought out by several national audience surveys. According to "Doordarshan 1995", while there are about 30 million television homes in urban areas, only about 15 million rural homes own sets and only 14 per sent rural population is served with television programmes. In case of Doordarshan's metro channel, the recorded urban and rural viewership is 65 and 9 per cent, respectively. It will perhaps not be wrong to aver that it is hard for any state communication policy to easily bridge this hiatus.

The question, therefore, arises : should government alone be entrusted with the task of looking for a widely accepted and equitably prepared communication policy? Probably not. This is perhaps why that, being prompted by such considerations, the I&B ministry, prepared the questionnaire on media policy. However, what should be the broad parameters and long-term objectives of a balanced communication policy? Let us attempt to answer this proposition.

In the first instance, it should be clearly stated that it is almost impossible to have a rigid, pre-determined or uncompromising agenda or charter for media programming. Secondly, it would be appropriate and prudent to outline only loose, general and liberal guidelines for communication planners. What is, however, really vital is overall harmony between vision and national perspectives of history, nationalism, heritage, social and political systems, regional and national aspirations, identity and basic current compulsions. A sense of unity, concern, relevance and togetherness should be reflected in the media what we get to read, listen or view day in and day out, for all ages, sexes, creeds and economic status.

What is, however, important to understand, appreciate and to concede is that not all that appears on the screens, radio sets, newspapers, or magazines would suit all tastes, ages, regions, sections, sexes. Everyone should have the liberty to choose what one likes. The freedom of choice is the basic democratic right. Media should have the capacity, willingness, urge and desire to satisfy as many viewers' demands and expectations as possible within the dimensions of the policy blue prints indicated earlier.

It may perhaps not be fair for the democratically operating media systems that we have in India to be chained within a set of strait-jacket rules and regulations stringently enforced, word for word. Moreover, there are separate and independent laws and rules for the press, radio, television, cable networks, cinema, performing arts, etc. As radio and television are at present state-owned systems with the government of India's promise to enforce the Prasar Bharati Act, hopefully popularly agreed and generally acceptable national electronic media policies would be drawn up soon.

There is an oft repeated criticism that the government-owned media so frequently put out commercials, sponsored or soap operas and serials which are sheer consumerist, only entertainment, art for art's sake, and, therefore, should be abhorred. True, to some extent. But realistically speaking, it is an erroneous thinking. For, after all, such fare also has some messages—developmental, moral, social, educative or popular entertainment. Is entertainment also not necessary in the context of the tension-ridden modern work culture? To be able to entertain is also an art which has grown with human growth and progress.

What in reality shapes the communication policies are national considerations, local politics and a lot of other factors. Besides, it is the legislation, laws, rules, committee reports, regulations and parliamentary announcements and court pronouncements that determine a nation's communication policies. As for the international communications flow impacting a nation's policies, no appropriately structured or pre-determined parameters can be prescribed, foreseen or assumed. This indeed is an extremely grey area.

In a majority of the western communication systems, the state's role is minimal; actually not beyond defence, security or national integrity limits vis-a-vis communication. In Sweden, for example, mass media are guaranteed "a diversified flow of information, and the state has limited its role in media operations." Both in the US and UK, the state role in mass media is almost invisible in normal times. In Australia and New Zealand also, media industry has predominant voice in taking independent decision.

No official communication policies have been issued in most western countries. The most important reason for such a state of affairs is believed to be, as a British media expert Anthony Smith, remarked some time ago, " a future-oriented communication policy is impossible."

However, the general trends towards deregulation and competition in industry make it impossible and inevitable to lay down in black and white rules and regulations to say what is fit or unfit for nation-wide dissemination with free market economy and market-place of ideas now ruling the roost. To issue any dicktats for media functioning is looked at with some kind of derision and general disfavour. Though setting out common parameters on the nation's communication policies may not be practicable and feasible, the fact is that as the revolution in communication technology is gripping the world at large, nations are willy-nilly being forced to examine and re-examine their own values, goals, economic, cultural and political pressures to pay more attention to the political role of communication policies is shaping the future national alternatives.

Communication policies of the future will, therefore, have to be driven the world over, by and large, besides a lot of other factors, increasingly by competition, controversy and confrontation. In India also, these factors will have tremendous influence in setting up our communication policy legistics.

Again, to quote Anthony Smith : "Communication policy has been subjected so much to the political dog-fight that institutions can survive only if they promise both sides of parliament that change would bring more trouble than stasis."

The statement fits on the situation in India like hand in glove. It is time India designed some sort of communication policy. Since it has to be a dynamic programme, national consensus will be necessary. Though this will take time and it may be after a lot of prevarication that such a character would be prepared. Once drawn up, this will have to be kept under a constant scrutiny and changes will have to be incorporated quickly as and when deemed necessary and proper.

2

TELEVISION POLICY — FREEDOM OF AIRWAVES

Rajeshwar Dyal

The first serious effort to formulate a comprehensive Television Policy was the Akash Bharti Report 1978, submitted by the Working Group on Autonomy for Akashvani and Doordarshan, constituted under the Chairmanship of Mr. B. G. Verghese. The Report, apart from being a comprehensive document on various facets of the working of radio and television in India also provided for a simple statute establishing the National Broadcast Trust, and setting out its objectives, scope, powers and basic structure. It was, at that point of time, hoped that the Akash Bharti Act establishing the National Broadcast Trust would come into force from 1 January 1979 and Akashvani and Doordarshan will cease to be the "attached offices" of the Ministry of Information and Broadcasting.

The Working Group in the concluding paragraph of its report had stated :

> The conferring of "full autonomy" on a sensitive organ of information, public opinion and cultural expression is a unique act of self abnegation on the part of a government and there is no doubt that the "transfer of power" to a national broadcast trust will be complex and delicate process.

It is by now, well known as to how the first effort undertaken to legislate for an autonomous broadcasting organization could not make headway due to political exigencies and lack of commitment on the part of political leadership.

It was not for another twelve years, that the Parliament in 1990, enacted the Prasar Bharati (Broadcasting Corporation of India) Act, 1990. The Act provided for the establishment of a Broadcasting Corporation of India. A unique feature of the Act was that it enlarged the definition of broadcasting, Section 2(c) as under :

> Broadcasting means the dissemination of any form of communication like signs, signals, writing, pictures, images and sounds of all kinds by transmission of electromagnetic waves through space or through cables intended to be received by the general public either directly or indirectly through the medium of relay stations and all its grammatical variations and cognate expressions shall be construed accordingly.

It is more comprehensive because it takes care of the transmission of electromagnetic waves through space or through cables. The Prasar Bharti Act aimed at creating a Broadcasting Corporation for India and the parameters within which this corporation was supposed to function. The Act provided a direction and pointer which should govern our broadcasting policies. Under Section 12(2) it was stated that the Broadcasting Corporation envisaged under the Act would be functioning and be guided by objectives such as :

> Upholding the unity and integrity of the country and the values enshrined in the Constitution, safeguarding the citizen's rights to be informed freely, paying special attention to the fields of education, literacy, agriculture, environment, etc. providing adequate coverage to the diverse cultures, informing and stimulating the national consciousness in regard to the status and problems of women, promoting social justice, safeguarding the rights of the working classes, serving the rural and weaker sections, providing suitable programmes keeping in view the special needs of minorities and the tribal communities, taking special steps to protect the interests of children, the blind, the aged and the handicapped, and other vulnerable sections of the people, promoting national integration, providing comprehensive broadcast coverage through the choice of appropriate technology, promoting research and development activities in order to ensure that radio and television broadcasting technology are constantly updated, expanding broadcasting facilities by

establishing additional channels of transmission at various levels, etc.

I have only presented a summary of the objectives contained in the Act. The Act, in terms of Section 14(1) also provided for the establishment of the Broadcasting Council, to receive and consider complaints.

From any person or group of persons alleging that a certain programme or broadcast or the functioning of the Corporation in specific cases or in general is not in accordance with the objectives for which the Corporation is established.

— and to advise the Corporation in the discharge of its functions in accordance with the objectives set out in Section 12.

According to Section I(3) of the Act, "it shall come into force on such date as the Central Government, may, by notification appoint." That notification, the Central Government has not issued for the last five years thus negating all efforts and the purpose for which the Act was passed by the Parliament.

3. — Public Rules the Air Waves
   — Freedom, One step closer
   — Freeing the Electronic Media from Shackles

This is how the Supreme Court of India ruling delivered on 9 February 1995 on air waves was widely hailed. Since the landmark judgement of the Supreme Court, holding that air waves and frequencies were public property and asking the Central Government to establish an independent, autonomous, public authority to regulate their use; lays down important guidelines for Broadcast Law, and also enlarges the scope of Section 19(1) of the Indian constitution, a detailed discussion of the judgement would be in order. The judgement, interalia, refers to : Freedom of Speech and expression—includes right to acquire and disseminate information, right to communicate through any media : print, electronic or audiovisual; Greater impact of TV on Society—Cannot afford basis for additional restrictions over and above those permissible under Article 19(2).

While resolving the litigation between the Cricket Association of Bengal (CAB) and Doordarshan over uplinking of self-generated signals to a foreign satellite for viewers abroad, the Court in its trend setting verdict delivered by a three-judge bench headed by Mr. Justice P. B.

Sawant said that it was the fundamental right of the telecaster to "educate" the viewers of the game, to watch the telecast was the viewers' sacred right to be entertained. An organiser like the CAB or the BCCI, could not be placed in the same scale as the business organizations wanting to make a large profit by telecasting the series.

One of the issues discussed in these judgements is the content of the freedom of speech and expression guaranteed by Article 19(1) (a) of the Constitution. There is unanimity that the right to receive and impart information is implicit in free speech and that cricket, like any other sports event, provides entertainment which is a facet of free speech. Both judgements emphasize that it is the right of the viewers and listeners which is paramount from the stand point of Article 19(1)(a).

There is a difference of opinion over whether the right of access to air waves/frequencies can be claimed as a fundamental right by an Indian citizen. According to Justices Sawant and Mohan : The freedom of speech includes the right to disseminate information to as wide a section of the population as is possible, and, therefore, the access which enables the right to be so exercised is also an integral part of the said right. The wider range of circulation of information or its greater impact cannot restrict the content of the right nor can it justify its denial. The virtues of the electronic media cannot become its enemies.

This right can be restricted but only on the grounds mentioned in Article 19(2) of the Constitution, namely, the sovereignty and integrity of India, the security of the state, friendly relations with foreign states, public order, decency or morality, contempt of court, defamation or incitement to an offence.

However, because the air waves are public property and are limited, there is an inbuilt "limitation imposed by the nature of the public property involved in the use of the electronic media". Consequently, they have to be used in the best interest of the society and this can be done either by a central authority establishing its own broadcasting network or regulating the grant of licenses to other agencies including the private agencies.

The judgement unanimously lays down that, "monopoly over broadcasting whether by government or by anybody else, is inconsistent with the free speech, right of the citizens. It is rightly emphasized by Justice Reddy that "state control really means governmental control, which, in turn, means control of the political party or parties in power for the time being. Such control is bound to colour the views, information and opinions conveyed by the media". The unanimous conclusion is that "the broadcasting media should be under the control of the public as distinct from government... It should be operated by a public statutory corporation or corporations, as the case may be, whose constitution and composition must be such as to ensure its/their impartiality in political, economic and social matters and on all other public issues. It/they must be required by law to present news, views and opinions in a balanced way ensuring pluralism and diversity of opinions and views. It/they must provide equal access to all the citizens and groups to avail of the medium."

> Suggesting changes in the Indian Telegraph Act, 1885, which at present governs the electronic media in the country, Mr. Justice Reddy said that the Act was intended for an altogether different purpose when it was enacted. This is the result of the law in this country not keeping pace with the technological advances in the field of information and communications. Therefore, Mr. Justice Reddy suggested, it was imperative that the Parliament makes a law placing the broadcasting media in the hands of a public body. "This is necessary to safeguard the interests of public and the interests of law as also to avoid uncertainty, confusion and consequent litigation", Mr Justice Reddy observed.

The Supreme Court has held that the rights of viewers are paramount; that they must participate in the affairs of the country and for that to happen they must be well informed. Says the judgement : One sided information, disinformation, misinformation and non-information, all equally create an uninformed citizenry which makes democracy a farce when the medium of information is monopolised either by a partisan central authority or by private individuals or oligarchic organizations. The answer lies in setting up of a public authority "representative of all sections of society and free from control of both the government as well as influential sections of society". The court also warned against government monopoly being replaced by that of powerful private broadcasters.

Implications of the Judgement

The Supreme Court Judgement has opened up exciting possibilities. Private sports casters would be allowed to buy rights from sports organizations and beam events alive, other broadcasters would have opportunity to present live news and current affairs programmes. It is felt that the judgement will eventually pave the way for the live telecast from India of programmes relating to entertainment and sports, as long as frequencies are available and Article 19(2) of the Indian Constitution is not violated.

Commenting on the judgement Amit Agarwal says : If the judgement is implemented in letter and spirit, it could lead to a new era in private broadcasting. It should be possible for political parties to buy time on private channels and telecast live speeches by their leaders. Similarly, Indian broadcasters will now have the right to telecast live entertainment and sports programmes, even if they are guided by commercial considerations, (*India Today*, March 15 1995).

Notwithstanding the assurances of the government to set up new public authority fairly quickly (Bhaskar Ghose, *Ibid*), frankly I see no great hope of Doordarshan getting its autonomy. In another seminar held at Bangalore in early September, Mr. Ghose stated that a comprehensive Broadcasting Act will regulate satellite channels and allow private satellite channels to uplink from within the country; however, there is no reference to the autonomy being granted to Doordarshan, which will continue to be a major player in the context of T.V. programming in India.

It will be pertinent to refer to, in passing the Draft Bill for Media Autonomy prepared by the Centre for Media Studies. The Draft Bill claims to be a "comprehensive" legislation on Broadcasting and could cover Radio, Television, Satellite, Cable, Interactive T.V. multimedia, Terrestrial including MMDS and the Telegraph Act as relevant to Broadcasting.

The CMS Draft Bill provides for :

(1) An autonomous Broadcasting Commission of India (BCI) with responsibility for licensing operators.
(2) Prasar Bharati Corporation.
(3) Two councils on statutory footing, one for ensuring standard in broadcasting and other for promoting audience involvement and examination of complaints from public.
(4) Two Boards for coordinating cable, satellite and other channels, and other for coordinating community service broadcasting.

The Draft Bill provides for Advertising and Programme Codes applicable for all the three streams of broadcasting in the country, responsibility resting with the Standards Council.

The Cable Television Network (Regulation) Act, 1995 was intended to achieve three objectives : Cable operators are now legal and have three years period at their disposal to upgrade their systems to specifications.

The bill which is pending presidential assent makes it mandatory for cable operators to adhere to the prescribed programme and advertisement code. Whereas, it is yet to be seen as to how effective implementation of the Bill would be particularly with reference to applicability of codes and inspection by officers of the Central Government; the legislation is, as one media commentator put it; "like a speed breaker at the entrance to an information super high way". However, with the entry of big players in the cable TV industry, and poor infrastructure, the industry presents a chaotic market. Licenses and permissions are not forthcoming in spite of the Cable TV Act, which says that each state government will have to evolve a policy on how the cables are to be laid.

In this brief overview of the current state of broadcasting legislation, some important features stand out :

(1) Quality of T.V. Programmes
(2) Lack of Television Policy

Quality of TV Programmes

It was indeed startling to know that the Chairman of the National Human Rights Commission, Mr. Ranganath Misra sought the support of the United Nations in dealing with violence on television. Speaking recently on the activities of the Commission at the Centre for Strategic and International Studies in Washington, Mr. Mishra said that he had written to the US Secretary General Mr. Boutros Ghali on the subject of violence on television which militated against the concept of human rights. He said his commission was trying to stop projection of violence on the Indian television, but foreign television shows, now available in the country, depicted violence in a big way.

Lack of Television Policy

In a seminar held recently at Kuala Lumpur on, Asian Values in Journalism, the Foreign Minister of Malaysia in his inaugural address, gave two examples of trivialising our cultural traditions by foreign T.V. networks and both the examples were from India : the abusive expression used against Mahatma Gandhi in the STAR television programme hosted by Nikki Bedi; and the newsclip of cows straddling the Bombay streets shown on the occasion of the launching of CNN Doordarshan agreement. In both cases, sensitivities of the Indian viewers were deeply hurt. These instances were not the only one which have evoked concern and unhappiness about the values that the Indian television tends to foster. Media analysts and commentators have pointed to the country lacking a TV policy which would promote relevant, good quality programmes while discouraging competitive mindlessness and vulgarity.

In this free-for-all scenario, there has been a steady deterioration in the quality of most programmes. The President of the Cable Operators Association, Roopa Sharma says, she receives more and more complaints about explicitly sexual sequences included in programmes for universal distribution. Most entertainment channels are slaves to glitzy western consumerism and sex and violence themes.

India is increasingly becoming the playing field of the world's biggest media players for their share of our unregulated 15 million homes cable TV market run by 60,000 operators. This market is bigger than that of any country in Europe barring Russia and Germany.

The Ministry of Information and Broadcasting and Doordarshan are just not bothered. Rather than encouraging and producing good quality programmes Doordarshan claims to break new ground by doubling its viewer ratings and income by retransmitting filmy trash.

Television in India has failed to offer any perspective on information, education or entertainment. Information is reduced to entertainment, and the latter to triviality. The mandate of television is not to make super-profits, but to make good programmes.

In one of his leading articles, Parful Bidwai says :

> What we need is a comprehensive policy to promote high-quality, independent, credible and competent television, which is at least as good as our press. This can only be done if DD is replaced by an independent authority and restructured so that professionals replace bureaucrats and sycophants. Its newsroom must be placed under the control of a neutral body of well trained journalists. It should be mandated to promote quality entertainment.

Communication system decisions made today will affect what will be available fifty years hence. It is, therefore, imperative that everywhere the broadcasting policy and broadcasting laws are geared to serve the society for the greatest good of the largest number of people. That should be the vision and the philosophy permeating our broadcast media.

3

PUBLIC SERVICE BROADCASTING IN INDIA — EXPERIENCES AND ISSUES

Sunil Misra ·

The Concept

Programmes over mass media which are of utility to the common men fall within the purview of Public Service Broadcasting. These could be in the form of announcements forewarning natural calamities, information on disaster management, weather reports, programmes on agriculture, market rates, health, family planning or population education, or the broadcasts on civic and social issues, highlighting peoples' problems, legal advice, making people aware of their rights, environmental pollution, and development support programmes. Public Service Broadcasting also includes programmes on national integration, communal harmony and maintaining peoples' morale during the contingencies. The programmes could be targetted to specific audience groups like women, youth, adolescents, students, farmers, industrial workers, etc., or could be broadcast for general audiences. Public Service Broadcasting is essentially a social service with the primary purpose of catering to the issue based information needs of the people. Considering the wide variety of life styles and ethno-cultural-linguistic divergences, the programmes have to be culturally compatible and according to the tastes, expectations and intellectual status of the target audience. Such programmes are expected to transcend the barriers of illiteracy and poverty and reach those groups of people who otherwise do not have much access to other direct sources of information. In Public Service Broadcasting, the commitments for development and welfare of the people take precedence over the commercial interests of the media.

Public Service Broadcasts can broadly be classified into information oriented and action oriented broadcasts. The former relate to education and sensitisation of the audiences on different issues of public interest. The latter envisage galvanising people for positive follow up action. Development support communication generally falls in the latter category.

The objectives and contents of the programme determine the format of Public Service Programmes. In the past messages have been successfully communicated using formats like soap opera, serialised plays, interviews, straight talks, discussions, public hearing over media, out-door broadcasts and by inviting selected members of the audiences to present their view points on the public interest issues. Tele-conferencing or radio bridge programmes are the latest introduction to the formats of Public Service Broadcasting.

The Social Setting

India is a large country inhabited by 4635 castes and communities spread over 91 eco-cultural zones (Source : Anthropological Survey of India). There are 18 national languages and around 200 major dialects. On attaining independence, India was confronted with massive problems of diverse origin and nature. A large and heterogenous population, a stagnant economy, communal conflicts, caste distinctions, exploitation of weaker sections and an administrative machinery which was more familiar with governing a subject nation than development of the people. These problems were further compounded by the fact that a large majority of people had low aspirations and expectations from life. They had limited mental horizons and traditionally, had not enjoyed any political, social and economic rights. The foremost task, therefore, was to transform this large but inert population from being passive witnesses of the programmes of planned social and economic change to becoming conscious partners in the process of nation building. This also involved galvanising social institutions to become dynamic forces to keep pace with the dynamics of technological and planned social change. Around 75 per cent of India's population lives in villages and, therefore, primary focus of the education and sensitisation process had to be the mass base of rural population.

Indian villages have generally been described as "self contained little universe" in which different groups in the hierarchy are bound by a symbiosis of social relations. Each of these groups is obliged to perform its traditionally determined social and economic functions for the other groups and get remunerated according to the prefixed norms. The professional specialisation in the gamut of group determined occupations, which are also arranged in a hierarchical order in the total occupational structure of the society, provide scope for development within the given social framework. The caste and community status is generally associated with the occupation and this, in turn, determines the pattern of inter-group behaviour. Social stratification and hierarchical ranking of the occupations ensures economic and social protection, promotes professional excellence and also, to an extent, eliminates clash of interests among different groups. In this manner, not only conflicts and competition is minimised but survival of different groups is also assured.

For centuries, this arrangement contributed to sustenance of Indian village communities as close knit cohesive societies. On the other hand, this also insulated them from extraneous influences and thereby resistant to change. Generally speaking, life in Indian rural communities can be characterised by poverty, illiteracy and limited mental horizons. For nearly half of the population, living below poverty line or on the fringe of it, development is not a priority in life and survival takes precedence over it. In such a situation, people tend to seek security within their own groups and avoid even minimal conflict with their social and physical environment. They are more inclined to maintain status quo than make a conscious effort to change. On the other hand, every mediated change brings in an element of crisis within the group. It involves adoption of new behaviour, evolution of new relationships, introduction of new kind of specialisation and even emergence of new leadership. The conflicts take place because the established order feels threatened with the new practices. The communication strategies for change including Public Service Broadcasting, as such, have to be sensitive to such issues which directly have an effect on the level of people's conscious participation in a programme.

Historical Perspective

Broadcasting in India, since its inception, has been used as an instrument of social change. In the initial stages, radio broadcasts used to have two major components, namely, entertainment and information. Subsequently, educational broadcasts, both formal and non-formal, were introduced. In the post independence era, a number of new services in the realm of public service broadcasting were started by the All India Radio. These included Farm and Home Broadcasts, Health and Family Welfare Planning related programmes, Formal and Non-Formal Education, and broadcasts on popular science, civic and social issues. The programmes for the special audiences, such as, women, youth, adolescents, agriculturists, tribals, industrial workers, armed forces, etc., were mainly composite programmes with a mixture of light entertainment, music and education and information. Social issues as relevant to respective target audiences were also taken up in such programmes. In order to provide a forum for discussing peoples' problems. Public participation programmes were started by many radio stations. Though the format of presentation differed from one radio station to the other, the primary emphasis was on highlighting the problems and grievances of individual listeners.

Television in India started as a medium for educational broadcasts in 1959. In 1975-76, the Satellite Instructional Television Experiment (SITE) was taken up to apply sophisticated satellite communication technology for social education and rural development for the people living in remote and backward regions. In the initial stages, a large chunk of the television transmission time was devoted to development support programmes and in dealing with civic or social issues. In the later stages, while radio maintained its development, information and education oriented stance, television, to an extent, drifted to become an extended arm of the film industry. A point that merits attention at this stage is that effectiveness of medium of mass communication is basically contingent on the image it acquires in the eyes of the people. This, in turn, influences peoples' judgement and expectations from the medium. In the current mass media scenario, while radio is still accepted as the medium for public service and development, television is looked for programmes of light entertainment. Perhaps commercial considerations and competition from purely entertainment oriented multiple channel cable television, forced the Indian television to follow the popular trends. It is noteworthy in this context that there would always be a gap between the potential of a medium of mass communication and its actual utilisation within the given social situation. Being an audiovisual medium, television has the greatest potential of influencing public opinion and in mobilising grass root level organisations. However, because of a number of factors including political compulsions, administrative ethos and the operational realities, its inherent strengths as public service medium could seldom be fully utilised. Technology is not the master but a means to achieve certain ends. On the other hand, the political, social, economic and cultural institutions as well as the latent needs of the society determine the growth and application of technology. Radio has, however, all along played a significant role in the realms of Public Service Broadcasting.

Public Service Programmes

Both radio and television have a long history of Public Service Broadcasting. It would be practically impossible to list out the whole range and variety of Public Service Programmes put out by both the media. However, in the following paragraphs, a few selected programmes are described by way of illustration.

1. Satellite Instructional Television Experiment (SITE) was launched for a period of one year between August 1975 and July 1976. The main aim was to reach the messages on development and create awareness about the social issues among the people living in the remote and backward regions. The experiment was simultaneously launched in 2400 selected villages of six states of the country where community viewing television sets were installed. This was a unique experiment in the sense that for the first time sophisticated satellite communication technology was used for Public Service.
2. Health Hints over Radio, are put out for a period of five minutes every day. An eminent doctor is invited to discuss common health issues and diseases, their prevention and cure. These broadcasts became so popular that a voluntary group of health practitioners in Delhi obtained their scripts and published them in a book form. There is also considerable audience support to these programmes.
3. Radio has a history of broadcasting to the rural people. The programmes generally include entertainment, information and some hard core broadcasts for the farmers. These programmes enjoy considerable audience patronage as brought out various audience research studies. In the southern states of the country, a new variety of rice was introduced over radio. It had a very wide acceptance and came to be popularly known as the radio rice in the states of Tamil Nadu and Karnataka.
4. In order to promote active participation of the people in the radio broadcasts, thousands of rural radio forums were established in different states. Community sets were installed in the selected villages where people were made to collect at the fixed hour and listen to the rural broadcasts. The local development functionary was also made to attend these fora and answer the queries from the listeners. In case he was not able to deal with them, the members of the rural radio forum were encouraged to send them

to the broadcasting station for appropriate response in the subsequent programmes. These forums, however, faded out after successfully working for a number of years.

5. Mention may also be made of the Public Participation programmes regularly put out by several radio stations. In these programmes, people are encouraged to write about their grievances on the civic or social issues or even seek legal advice. These are compiled and forwarded to the concerned authority in the Government or other agencies. Their responses are then broadcast over radio. In one of the states, the Chief Minister himself participated in these programmes once in a month. These programmes enjoy considerable audience support.

Basic Issues

Considering the socio-cultural divergences and the wide variety of region specific developmental issues, the Public Service Broadcasting has to be taken up at the micro-level. The Public Service programmes are likely to have far greater acceptance if they address to specific information needs of the local population. This imperatively calls for setting up local broadcasting station for a small area. The advantage is that the programmes can be devised in a manner that the audience in its primary service area identify it as their own station. However, this would be possible only if far greater proportion of programmes are based on peoples' participation. In this respect television mainly relies on network broadcasting through its large number of relay transmitters. Thus, a majority of people are forced to watch Hindi programmes originating from Delhi. The All India Radio has established a large number of local stations to cater to the population of a smaller area. However, because of the factors like limited transmission time, over centralisation in deciding about the programme fare and lack of specialisation among the staff to undertake the challenge of local broadcasting, these stations have, by and large, followed the programme pattern of the main stations.

It is a well known fact that majority of the radio coverage in the country is through single channel medium wave stations. Therefore, the programmes have to be of composite nature catering to the tastes of a variety of the audience groups. Besides, the stations also have to conform to the policy directives and instructions from the central broadcasting organisation and the Ministry of Information and Broadcasting. With the result, they enjoy very little flexibility in programming; as a corollary, there is considerable straitjacketing of the programme fare over both radio and television. One consequence of this approach has been that the programme cadre lacks specialisation and is full of generalists.

Public Service Broadcasting depends upon identification of crucial issues and critical areas for action. In other words, effective programmes can only be produced on an accurate data base and system to regularly provide feed back on the needs and demands of the audiences. However, this has been the most neglected area as programmes are put out in a routine manner. Some times, the subject matter specialists are invited or the liaison is maintained with the concerned departments. However, this has been too inadequate since most of the specialists are not fully aware of the ground realities and the departmental representatives do not have access to the latest information on the subject. Inspite of these handicaps, however, people to a great extent rely on the broadcasting organisations for their need based information requirements.

The primary aim of Public Service Broadcasting is to improve the quality of life of the people; also to legitimate the introduction of new ideas and behaviours. In the Indian situation, the broadcast media have to maintain a balance between popular tastes and the demands of the Governmental agencies. In this tight rope walking, the balance invariably tilts in the favour of the latter at the cost of the audience interests. The experience has shown, that properly researched programmes have had considerable impact on the people. It is only in the case of lack of need synchronisation and over emphasis on programme specific communication, that audience lose interest and look for alternate sources.

4

INDIA NEEDS A FILM POLICY—NOW, MORE THAN EVER BEFORE

Jag Mohan

In making this demand that India needs a Film Policy now than ever before, possibly, I could be the 101st person or institution during the first century of the Cinema. Now and then, committees and working groups have been set up. Reports have been prepared and submitted to the Ministry of Information and Broadcasting or placed before the Parliament. And then, the saddest thing that has most often happened is that the reports have been shoved under the carpet or consigned to the file rack to gather dust or to be eaten away by silverfish. This is not to deny that off and again, some major recommendations have been implemented and much good also has accrued out of such implementation to the nation.

First Policy Report

It is a worthwhile exercise to review the major and important efforts in this direction for that will enable all those concerned to chart out a course of action in the second century of the Cinema that has just begun. All the more so, because the role of the film in the changed media scenario, with TV dominating, has to be re-assessed and re-defined.

The earliest attempt to understand cinema as such and to evolve a policy was made by the erstwhile British rulers of India way back in 1927. They set up what is known as the Indian Cinematograph Committee, under the chairmanship of Diwan Bahadur T. Rangachariar, an eminent lawyer from Madras.

True to their imperialist preoccupations and policies, the Britishers wanted to come "face to face" with cinema as a mass medium. They also wanted to protect their "Empire Films", at a time when American films were having the monopoly of cinema halls and the nascent Indian feature films then called "bioscope" and the short film "topicals" had a tendency to reflect nationalist aspirations for independence.

The Rangachariar Committee travelled "9400 miles in India, visited production centres and theatres, questioned 353 witnesses and studied 320 replies to the 4,325 questionnaires sent out and spent Rs. 1,93,000." As a result of this laborious effort, a one-volume report and four volumes of "Evidences" were published. The main report had also included a "Minute of Dissent" by the three British members.

The report of the Indian Cinematograph Committee found that the censorship rules were adequate and that there was no need for any "imperial preference" to British films. It was of the opinion that on the whole the films shown in India did not bring "Western society into contempt" nor did they "undermine Indian respect for Western women." The report endorsed the growing Indian film industry's demand for more facilities and encouragement through the abolition of duty on unexposed "raw-stock" imported from abroad and reduction of entertainment tax.

The Committee also recommended that there should be a Central Censor Board and the State Boards should be abolished. For the first time, the Committee suggested that films should be classified as "U" for universal exhibition and "P" for "parents" only and not for children. The ultimate result was that the British Government ignored the report and set the trend of pushing reports under the carpet.

After Independence

India's first Prime Minister, Jawaharlal Nehru, was a many-sided person, who was not daunted by the traumatic experiences of the partition of the country and the assassination of Mahatma Gandhi in the early years of independence. It was he, who set up the Sahitya Akademi, Sangeet Natak Akademi and the Lalit Kala Akademi to promote literature, performing arts and the visual arts, respectively, having seen such institutions in foreign countries.

The Information Films of India, started by the British to promote the war effort and closed down after independence, was revived as the Films Division. Nehru also set up the Film Enquiry Committee under the chairmanship of S. K. Patil, a Congress leader of Bombay and a member of the Constituent Assembly. This was in response to the demand from the film industry. Besides, Nehru believed that films had great influence "in moulding the people of the country, with an influence greater than that of newspapers and books, all combined."

Yet another major contribution of Nehru was that he requested Devika Rani to organise a broad-based seminar on films in 1955 at New Delhi, which ultimately turned out to be the "mother of all film seminars", in India, with eminent film personalities attending it. The proceedings came out in a handsome book, that had great influence on those, who frequented the corridors of power. It was at Nehru's behest that the Children's Film Society was started in 1955.

The S. K. Patil Film Enquiry Committee Report had a positive impact, with the result that several worthwhile institutions and beneficial practices were initiated. The Committee, set up in August 1949, had apart from S. K. Patil several eminent persons as its members, V. Shantaram of Prabhat, B. N. Sircar of New Theatres, two Members of the Constituent Assembly, a professor of history and a representative of the Ministry of Information and Broadcasting.

The Committee in its report released in 1951 not only went into the growth and organisation of the film industry but also indicated the lines of future development. It suggested specific measures for the encouragement and promotion of films in India. Among its major recommendations were :

1. Setting up of a government-funded film financing corporation to help talented and "genuine" film-makers.
2. Founding of an "Institute of Film Art" for the training of film technicians, directors and actors.
3. Setting up of a Film Council of India with proper representation of the industry to regulate and supervise the growing industry.
4. Formation of an Export Corporation for Indian films to foreign countries with concentration of people of Indian origin.
5. Manufacture of raw film in India, as also film equipment.
6. Institution of annual cash awards for films of outstanding merit as an incentive.
7. Abolition of octroi duties, internal customs duties, police charges, etc.
8. Creation of two categories for censorship certificates for films— "U" for unrestricted universal exhibition and "A" for adult films.

Delayed Implementation

The scheme of State Awards for best films in Hindi and regional languages as also for documentaries and children's films were enunciated in 1954 and the first lot for the films of 1954 was given in 1955.

In 1960, the Film Finance Corporation, a public sector undertaking to provide finance at reasonable rates to raise the standard of films was inaugurated (It was merged with the National Film Development Corporation).

In 1961, the Film Institute of India was set up in Poona (now Pune), in the extensive grounds and buildings of the Prabhat studios. Later Television was included and it became Film and Television Institute of India.

In 1963, the Indian Motion Picture Export Corporation was started. Much later, its business was amalgamated with that of the National Film Development Corporation. The Hindustan Photo Film Manufacturing Company, Ooty, a public sector undertaking started in 1960 has been supplying the raw film stock to film producers for over three decades and saving millions of rupees of foreign exchange.

The National Film Archive started in 1964 was a by-product of the increasing involvement of the Ministry of Information and Broadcasting in films, for which the initial thrust was given by the Patil Committee.

After the Patil Committee Report, there were Reports galore, usually mentioned in bibliographies of books. Among such Reports were :

1. Report on an Enquiry into the Conditions of Labour in the Cinema Industry in Bombay State 1956.
2. Report of the Society for the Prevention of Unhealthy Trends in Motion Picture, Vol. 1, 1959 and Vol. 2, 1961.
3. Report on Documentary Films and Newsreels of the Committee on Broadcasting and Information Media 1966.
4. Film Enquiry Committee Report (1962-63) of the Government of West Bengal 1968.
5. Report of the Enquiry Committee on Film Censorship (headed by G. D. Khosla) 1969.

Most of these reports were ignored and forgotten even though some of them were valuable and considerable amounts of money were spent on these Committees.

Interesting Developments

During the two decades between mid-1950s and mid-1970s, many interesting developments took place in the Indian film industry. From the alumni of the Film Institute emerged Mani Kaul, Kumar Shahani, Adoor Gopalakrishnan and Girish Kasaravalli among others as a new breed of directors. Out of the loans advanced by the Film Finance Corporation, some memorable films like Mrinal Sen's *Bhuvan Shome*, Basu Chatterji's *Sara Akash*, Trilok Jetly's *Godan*, Prem Kapur's *Andha Galli*, Adoor Gopalakrishnan's *Swayamvaram*, M. S. Sathyu's *Garam Hawa* constituting the New Wave.

Film Societies began proliferating with the Federation of Film Societies helping them in getting foreign classics. Marie Seton went on a tour of major cities giving lectures on film appreciation. Several film societies started bringing out magazines like "Close-up" and "Montage".

The National Film Festivals and International Film Festivals hosted by the Ministry of Information and Broadcasting put India on the world map.

Above all Satyajit Ray emerged as a "World Class" Indian film director with his Pather Panchali triology, Charulata and other films that had the distinctive stamp of his genius. Besides as the President of the Federation of Film Societies, from its inception till his death, he guided it in the correct direction.

More than all this, Indira Gandhi, as the Minister for Information and Broadcasting, and later as the Prime Minister, was keen that the Indian films should make qualitative improvement. Before she joined the Government of India, she was the Vice-President of the Film Federation of India and had rapport with Satyajit Ray as well as others like S. Sukhdev. It was she, who had invited Marie Seton to India. She encouraged innovations and her keen personal interest led to greater achievements.

Working Group for a Film Policy

A "Working Group on National Film Policy" was set up by the Government of India on the recommendation of a Conference of State Ministers of Information in 1979. K. Shivarama Karanth, Kannada writer, educationist and *Yaksha Gana* specialist was appointed as the Chairman. Among the members of his Working Group were Mrinal Sen, Shyam Benegal, Basu Bhattacharya, Adoor Gopalakrishnan, Ramanand Sagar and Manoj Kumar, Tarun Mazumdar (film-makers), Tarachand Barjatya and D. V. S. Raju (film producers), Dilip Jamdar (documentary film-maker), Vijaya Mulay (formerly of the Censor Board) and others.

The Report of the Working Group is by far the most comprehensive and need-based report, compiled so far in the history of India's cinema industry. It was the end-product of the collective effort of a group of idealistic and yet pragmatic cinema-minded persons.

It is 15 years since the Report came out but unlike the Patil Committee Report, nothing worthwhile emanated out of its recommendations. The Report is mentioned here and there, now and again, but to quote a film maker's comment, "It has been disowned by the governmental authorities and discarded by the industry." This may be considered uncharitable since the Report was of the "honest-to-goodness" grade, constructive and imaginative.

The Group endorsed the idea originally floated by the Federation of Film Societies long years ago when the late S. Sukhdev and late K. T. John, B. D. Garga and the present writer addressed a Federation meeting and suggested that like the three Akademis, a Chalachitra Akademi should be set up as the apex organization to look after the academic aspects of the cinema as an art form. The Working Group adopted the idea and expanded it by suggesting that the National Film Archives should come under the Akademi and that the later should oversee and regulate the policies and actions of all film-related institutions under the Ministry of Information and Broadcasting. The Group was keen to divest the National Film Development Corporation of some of its activities and take them over. The Group wanted a Research and Development Wing and a Film Documentation and Information Centre to be set up, as also a Film Museum in Delhi. It even went further and suggested ways and means of upgrading research in technology in Cinema equipment and of broad basing, and the production schedule of the Hindustan Photo Films in Ooty. It wanted to monitor the progress of the Film and Television Institution on a regular basis.

The State Film Awards too were to be handled by the Akademi just like what the other Akademis do. Like the Lalit Kala Akademi handling the Triennale Exhibition, the Chalachitra Akademi was to look after the Festivals.

In its enthusiasm, but correctly it said that cinema as such should be taken out of the State List of Subjects and transferred to the Union List or the Concurrent List.

The Working Group's ideas were bitterly contested by the various authorities of the institutions concerned. They did not want their powers to be truncated. They resented the idea of the Akademi overseeing their work and more so of shifting the venues from Pune, Bombay and elsewhere to Delhi. Some feared over-centralisation and a few even described it as a "Stalinist move", which was far from truth. All that the Working Group wanted was that the Chalachitra Akademi must be fusion of the British Film Institute and the American Motion Picture Academy of Arts and Science.

Apart from this, during the last few years technology has overtaken us with computers, satellite television, Internet, Information Highway and Cyberspace. Under this impact the Report, in a way, has become outdated.

The Government of India must act quick and fast for evolving a Film Policy for in 1997, we will have the 50th anniversary of the attainment of Independence and in 2000 A. D., we will be celebrating the Golden Jubilee of our Republic. The Government of India can make a historic present to the Indian Film Industry, which for the past decade has topped the list of film producing countries with USA and Japan coming next. Our nation deserves a better film industry and a Film Policy that can be implemented is what the industry deserves.

5

WOMEN AND MEDIA

Sharita Rai

A media policy for India, no matter how dynamic, can ill afford to focus media concerns in isolation from the integral development of the nation as a whole. It is in this context, therefore, that I would like to suggest that the women and media issue too, is not unrelated to the attributes of the larger focus of national development. Hence, the need to consider the relevant motive for articulating the women's development process with that of media planning and growth.

At the moment, needless to say, the two are quite separate, though perhaps simultaneous in their growth prospects vis-a-vis the impact of liberalisation and the era of market initiated development. However, this only underlines the need to align both processes—currently in the transition mode—to the common purpose of national endeavour.

First let's look at the media position. There is as yet no specific media policy in place. Even as the Comprehensive Broadcast Bill promises to deliver more private channels—both domestic and foreign, the broader media direction and structures are expected to be spelt out in the modified Prasar Bharati Bill, expected to come into force by year-end. Meanwhile "growth" continues unmediated and in arbitrary fashion.

The only tangibles are the available statistics and research projections. In a just-released report, *Mass Media and Marketing Communication : Prespectives into 2020*, Dr. N. Bhaskara Rao, founder Chairman of the Centre for Media Studies, and a media and market research expert, says that a certain alliance—expected sooner or later—between newspapers, television, radio, film, cable, music and multimedia among others, will make it one of the most influential industries of the country. The sector, thus dominated by monolithic corporate networks, is expected to grow from Rs. 10,000 crores today to Rs. 1,20,000 crores in the next two decades.

There will be a proliferation of television channels, but the print media will continue to be competitive, complementary and perhaps more credible than its electronic sibling. But, most importantly, as the media undergoes structural changes, media character too is expected to. "Media will become less of editing and more of designing" and the editor's role will continue to decline. The increased predominance of advertising will, therefore, in all probability turn mass media into a marketing media that is fragmented, targetted and niche oriented.

But, and here lies the moot point—despite the expected proliferation of media and the boom in the business, nearly one-fifth of the population would still be outside media.reach, even after 2010. And only ten per cent of the population will have on-line access to information. And this, in a country that is expected to have the highest number of TV households in the world by 2020 (a four to five-fold increase over the current 50 million households). In fact, by the year 2000 alone there will be 20 million households each with two TV sets!! the report says.

Proliferation, therefore, would not imply access for the general population. Only an enhanced access to markets and revenue that this major industry would be looking for. And the market research business which is also expected to expand ten-fold in the next two decades, will in all likelihood become yet another "equity" instrument, it is believed.

Software Requirement

In the context, software requirements will only be measured in quantitative and not qualitative terms. Projections show that software requirements would imply enhanced investments from the current Rs. 2000 crores to Rs. 20,000 crores by 2020. This, to meet the demand for increased hours of fresh programming that Indian TV would then require—which would be more than that of US TV by the year 2010. And the number of TV channels at this point, are expected to have stabilised at around 200.

There is of course, as yet, no move to quantify software needs in qualitative terms. Or more precisely, in socio-cultural and political contexts. As mentioned by several speakers in the consultation, including B. K. Chandrashekar and V. S. Gupta in the context of the Panchayati Raj institutions and their ability to "empower" women (and men) towards self-governance, there is, at the moment, little facility to assess the information needs of these members, as there is to create information processes that are part of a systems concept. The threat of sabotage, therefore, either by the hierarchy-driven political or social system, or even the market-driven private enterprise, is always imminent.

As of now, we merely have an entertainment model that is replication-oriented and dictated by the demands of the market. Film-based programmes, are, therefore, expected to sustain Indian TV for another decade. And thereafter, it is anticipated that there will be a reversal, with the demand for information based programmes taking over. But then, that's like anticipating the pot of gold at the end of the rainbow.

For the large majority of Indian women—both urban and rural—aspiring to look for life-sustaining survival options in an increasingly stressful, consumerist world, media development, the way it is headed today, has little to offer, either as information-related activity or as leisure. Little wonder then, that under the circumstances, the mental health of women—that most marginalised of population groups—has become a subject of urgent attention with consistent findings showing an increased prevalence of depression and related disorders. It has naturally become a serious cause of social anxiety particularly since it is often found to be related to her reproductive health and "larger life situation, particularly her role as mother." As light entertainment meanwhile, TV has less to offer than its predecessor—the theatre hall cinema. While research projections show that the cinema viewing public will grow, it also suggests that the cinema-going public will further decline by 2001. Clearly, there is little comparison between the cultural ritual of going to the cinema theatre, and viewing a film on TV. The one traditionally, has been known to have been a well-integrated social phenomenon with a built-in concept of leisure, while the other is no more than a merket-driven enterprise whose chief motive is to make profit out of the habit of consumption and excessive consumption at that!!

If there is one thing then, that the near-monopolistic electronic media—which TV has come to represent—has done, in the absence of appropriate software, is to further weaken the existing socio-cultural structures, without quite replacing it. So, while the rural woman could quite easily see in the "idiot-box" the natural panacea for a life of strife in which deprivation and alchoholism are regular bedfellows—without having too many expectations of it culturally, the urban woman must necessarily contend with the negatives in order to gain benefit from the "positives" that it offers.

Intrusive Medium—Disruption of Social Patterns

A notoriously intrusive medium, TV has, in the urban milieu, been the cause of various disruptions in the social pattern. And not always meaningfully.

And as yet, unpublished CMS study on the social impact of television, commissioned by DD concludes for instance that TV has accentuated the gaps in inter-spouse and parent children communication. The study spread across the five states of Andhra Pradesh, Assam, Maharashtra, Orissa and Uttar Pradesh, besides the cities of Delhi and Bangalore also adds that TV has blurred the distinctions between fiction and reality, especially in the case of children. It has also been persistently and persuasively negative in its portrayal of human behaviour so that crime and violence become portrayed as acceptable behaviour. While it has altered individual habits, it has also changed family habits such as bedtime and the play time of children. It has also drastically reduced the size of the reading public. Books, novels, magazines and daily newspapers—in that order—are the definite casualties.

Then, of course, there are other socio-cultural perceptions. According to the study, viewers across the country were emphatic in stating that the positive influences of TV far outweigh the negative. Referring naturally to the technology option, they cite "bringing the world closer", "increased consumer awareness" and "healthier competition in the market" among them, to support their view.

They are equally clear about the fact that television has helped increase "historical awareness" by which they meant the various mythology-based serials on DD and "cultural awareness" about people, places and traditions, besides better "political awareness" though current affairs programmes and news, do not figure high on most people's viewing list. The viewers have also expressed the view that TV has helped promote the folk traditions of our country. Only the educational programmes meant for children are reported to find a low viewership.

There can be only two ways of assessing these findings. Simply through the two questions—does the viewer perception—shorn of too many software options—accurately reflect the media role, or should media help create a bias in favour of developmental targets thus aiding towards the mainstreaming of the entire information process?

Mechanisms for Evaluating Software

This brings one to some important questions regarding the mechanisms for evaluating software. Should the methodologies used for market research in the case of consumer products and services also be used to direct the course of an influential instrument of social intervention such as the mass media? Should the viewer be treated more as a consumer—in which case the above mentioned study would be appropriate in validating demand projections—or should it aim to reflect fundamental value positions with which to help arm the viewer with the ability to discriminate, before arriving at value assumptions?

But of course the initiative for that must come from the Government or from the academic community. No entrepreneur interested in the profits of supply and demand is likely to be inclined towards such philanthrophy. Atleast not as yet.

Though the mainstream approach has been to focus software development around urban-centred issues and to serve the socio-cultural and political interests of the urban viewer, draft proposals suggesting modifications to the Prasar Bharati Bill include setting up studios around the country. The 40 member group that worked on the draft and which includes noted journalist B. G. Verghese has reportedly spelt out the need to set up not just studios but training centres in various parts of the country that would contribute towards the creation of trained human resource for software development. Currently, one can only witness such distorted growth as the mushrooming of 16 such training schools in Delhi alone, within one year. And most of them with little or no hands on experience to venture such an enterprise.

Meanwhile, the arbitrary and directionless growth of software is unlikely to serve the cause of women, in their emerging new role towards the start of the 21st century. Slogans like human rights, empowerment, mainstreaming, legal and political rights, besides participation in the country's economic growth are far from being translated in the media as reflections of an active reality. Even an international event like the UN Women's Conference at Beijing found little space in the Indian media, leaving it to the perceptual value positions of the western media, information processes in India have yet to acknowledge these developmental urges in the women's movement. Women's participation in the decision-making processes that go towards nation building is still just a slogan, even as the media has sought to play no role in it.

6

MEDIA POLICY AND WOMEN'S ISSUES

Nandini Prasad

The debate on whether to have or not have a media policy is an old one. Time and again, policies, often called guidelines have been framed for different media activities, but a comprehensive media policy encompassing a holistic approach has never been attempted. Perhaps, the idea of having guidelines, and not a definite policy, was to provide room for manoeuvering and manipulating the media according to the convenience of the powers that be. But, time has now come, that we as concerned citizens of a democratic nation, ensure that a media policy covering all aspects of media and communications is evolved, to strengthen democratic processes and pluralisation of media.

Rapid changes in information technology and their likely impact on communication and education, on the economy and above all on society is a matter of serious concern for all, and especially media and communications professionals. The reason for this concern is simple. In India, information technology advancements seem to have completely overshadowed the more important aspects of social implications. There appears to be a blind faith in adopting the latest communication technology, leading to a gap between the haves and have-nots. Only some corridors of information flow exist. Since most decisions are taken in isolation of target groups, media are neither target-oriented nor do they reflect the concerns of most persons. Policy-decisions regarding hardware are taken on the basis of availability of state-of-the-art, while the software is market-driven. Understandably, media in the private sector have commercial interests, but it is important for them also to adhere to the concept of social and developmental responsibility and media ethics.

While speaking of society and its overall development, women's empowerment and their full participation on the basis of equality in all spheres of society, including participation in the decision-making process and access to power, are fundamental for the achievement of equality, development and peace in this world. The empowerment and advancement of women, including the right to freedom of thought, conscience, religion and belief, contribute to the moral, ethical, spiritual and intellectual needs of women as well as men, individually or in the community, thereby guaranteeing them the possibility of realizing their full potential in society and shaping their lives in accordance with their own aspirations.

Women and the Media

India is experiencing a rapidly changing media environment. The new "communications revolution" with satellite broadcasting and other advances in technology cut across national boundaries, putting the media beyond the reach of Governments and social institutions such as the family and community.

While the globalization of the media offers the promise of greater interaction among peoples, it can also create and reinforce images, attitudes and behaviour that may often be contradictory to the advancement of women.

Among the most destructive forms of media influence is the perpetuation and reinforcement of negative images of women that do not provide an accurate or realistic picture of women's multiple roles and value in a changing world. Even more insidious is the use by the media of women's bodies as sex objects. Most vulnerable to the influence of the media are young women, who fell impelled to conform to the materialistic, consumer-driven and exploitative stereotypes. At the same time, while the media may have been used to promote cultural values, ideology and religion selectively to justify the control of women by social and State institutions, the progressive forms of cultural values and religion have also been effective means to promote the advancement of women at the grass-root levels. It is appropriate to change current media practices that thrive on sensationalism and profit motives, as otherwise the conflict between conservative values and pornographic and violent images can only worsen.

Media images of women affect women's lives in several ways : they perpetuate stereotypes and create a distorted self-image. Myths and misconceptions enforced by the media also affect the thinking and attitudes of government planners, thereby further marginalizing the role and contribution of women as well as compromising the future of young women and the girl-child.

Media ownership patterns indicate a strong link between business—especially multinationals—and political groups. At the same time, ownership and control of the media are in male hands, which means that the content of the media is presented largely from a male perspective, reflecting, in many ways, men's values and perceptions. While there are increasing numbers of women employed in the various media, employment patterns show that women are grossly under-represented in decision-making positions. The power to control and significantly influence the media still eludes women.

Women's Empowerment and Media : Fourth UN Conference on Women (Beijing, 1995)

Undoubtedly, media play a major role in the empowerment or disemployment of women and the framers of media policy need to pay due attention to this. Recognising this, the Fourth World Conference on Women held at Beijing in September 1995 devoted a separate section to "Women and the Media" in the final Declaration and Platform for Action adopted at the conclusion of the Conference. It clearly defined the significant role media needs to play in accelerating the process of advancement of women. The document noted :

> "During the past decade, advances in information technology have facilitated a global communication network that transcends national boundaries and has an impact on public policy, private attitudes and behaviour, especially of children and young adults. Everywhere the potential exists for the media to make a far greater contribution to the advancement of women.
>
> "More women are involved in careers in the communications sector, but few have attained positions at the decision-making level or serve on governing boards and bodies that influence media policy. The lack of gender sensitivity in the media is evidenced by the failure to eliminate the gender-based stereotyping that can be found in public and private local, national and international media organizations.
>
> "The continued projection of negative and degrading images of women in media communications—electronic, print, visual and audio—must be changed. Print and electronic media in most

countries do not provide a balanced picture of women's diverse lives and contributions to society in a changing world. In addition, violent and degrading or pornographic media products are also negatively affecting women and their participation in society. Programming that reinforces women's traditional roles can be equally limiting. The world-wide trend towards consumerism has created a climate in which advertisements and commercial messages often portray women primarily as consumers and target girls and women of all ages inappropriately. "Women should be empowered by enhancing their skills, knowledge and access to information technology. This will strengthen their ability to combat negative portrayals of women internationally and to challenge instances of abuse of the power of an increasingly important industry. Self-regulatory mechanisms for the media need to be created and strengthened and approaches developed to eliminate gender-biased programming. Most women, especially in developing countries, are not able to access effectively the expanding electronic information highways and, therefore, cannot establish networks that will provide them with alternative sources of information. Women, therefore, need to be involved in decision-making regarding the development of the new technologies in order to participate fully in their growth and impact.

"In addressing the issue of the mobilization of the media, Governments and other actors should promote an active and visible policy of mainstreaming a gender perspective in policies and programmes".

Action Points for Government : Recommendations of Fourth UN Conference on Women (Beijing, 1995)

The Beijing Declaration and Platform for Action enunciated the specific steps which governments of participating countries need to undertake. While evolving a national media policy, these suggestions assume great significance and need immediate attention of policy planners.

To ensure increase in participation and access of women to the media, various actions to be taken by the governments, as suggested at Beijing, included :

(a) Support women's education, training and employment to promote and ensure women's equal access to all areas and levels of the media;

(b) Support research into all aspects of women and the media so as to define areas needing attention and action and review existing media policies with a view to integrating a gender perspective;

(c) Promote women's full and equal participation in the media, including management, programming, education, training and research;

(d) Aim at gender balance in the appointment of women and men to all advisory, management, regulatory or monitoring bodies, including those connected to the private and State or public media;

(e) Encourage, to the extent consistent with freedom of expression, these bodies to increase the number of programmes for and by women to see to it that women's needs and concerns are properly addressed;

(f) Encourage and recognize women's media networks, including electronic networks and other new technologies of communication, as a means for the dissemination of information and the exchange of views, include at the international level, and support women's groups active in all media work and systems of communications to that end;

(g) Encourage and provide the means or incentives for the creative use of programmes in the national media for the dissemination of information of various cultural forms of indigenous people and the development of social and educational issues in this regard within the framework of national law;

(h) Guarantee the freedom of the media and its subsequent protection within the framework of national law and encourage, consistent with freedom of expression, the positive involvement of the media in development and social issues.

For promoting a balanced and non-stereotyped portrayal of women in the media, it suggested the following points of actions to be taken by the governments :

(a) Promote research and implementation of a strategy of information, education and communication aimed at promoting a balanced portrayal of women and girls and their multiple roles;

(b) Encourage gender-sensitive training for media professionals, including media owners and managers, to encourage the creation and use of non-stereotyped, balanced and diverse images of women in the media;

(c) Encourage the media to refrain from presenting women as inferior beings and exploiting them as sexual objects and commodities, rather than presenting them as creative human beings, key actors and contributors to and beneficiaries of the process of development;

(d) Promote the concept that the sexist stereotypes displayed in the media are gender discriminatory, degrading in nature and offensive;

(e) Take effective measures or institute such measures, including appropriate legislation against pornography and the projection of violence against women and children in the media.

Suggestions for Media Policy

To promote positive images of women in the media with a view to influencing, transforming and creating social environment policies affecting women, according women their rightful place in society as active and equal partners in development and enhancing women's dignity and self-image, the framers of media policy need to include the following :

1. To ensure that women enjoy greater access to all forms of communications technology, so that they become creators and producers and not merely recipients and consumers of media messages :

   (i) Women must be trained in the use of new technologies, by providing at least 30 per cent reservation of seats in institutions providing training in communications and media;

   (ii) All media organizations must have 30 per cent reservation for women in jobs at all levels, including decision-making levels;

   (iii) Encourage the use of alternative media specially by women in rural areas by organising training in communication techniques at the village level.

2. To change the gender orientation of the mainstream media and ensure the elimination of gender stereotyping in the portrayal of women in all forms of mass media :

(i) All journalism and mass communications training coursers run by various universities, institutions, organizations, etc. must have a capsule for gender;

(ii) All media professionals including media owners and managers must be trained in gender sensitivity to encourage the creation and use of positive images of women and men in the media.

(iii) To build an audience base of discerning consumers who will recognise gender stereotypes in the media and demand quality media output, media-awareness training must be popularised specially in schools and communities. For schools, it can be included as part of the curriculum; while the NGOs' co-operation can be sought for the communities.

(iv) A mechanism for media monitoring must be evolved by setting up an apex body at the national level which will coordinate and support the media monitoring efforts of women's and consumers' groups at the regional, state, district and town/village level. The apex body must include representatives from all sections of the society, and should not consist of only the elite and the intellectuals.

(v) The press laws must include appointing an ombudsperson exclusively for coverage of gender issues in all newspaper. The ombudsperson must enjoy an independent status.

(vi) Although the government has evolved a comprehensive code for advertising on radio and television, they pertain only to government media. Since this code is extensively violated, in the proposed mechanism for monitoring, scope for reportage of such violations will automatically increase.

Simultaneously, it must be ensured that violators are penalised and such violations are widely publicised. For avoiding inordinate delay in deciding the penalty through the existing legal system, special courts must be entrusted with this responsibility.

7

MEDIA POLICY AND NATIONAL DEVELOPMENT

Vir Bala Aggarwal

This paper examines the relevance of the media policy for the development of the country and underlines the issues which would shape, direct and dominate the development scenario in the coming decade. The question of laying down the national media policy has been engaging the attention of media scholars, Government functionaries and public persons for quite some time now.

The basic function of mass media is to provide information, education, instruction and entertainment to the people. The media also motivates people, directly or indirectly to discharge these functions in a meaningful and purposeful manner in any community. The media agencies should be clear about the broad communication objectives which may guide their operations in their day to day work.

There are numerous factors that determine the development of a country. The process of development in any specific country must also take into account the peculiarities specificities, the goals set by the policy makers and planners, the objectives limitations imposed by historical development of the social, economic, cultural and political structures and processes. We shall discuss these and the role of media policy as playing an effective and facilitative role in helping the process of development of a nation in general with special reference in the context of India. Before one discusses this and the complex relationships it creates, it is pertinent to discuss what is meant by development, since there is no agreement about this among planners and social thinkers.

According to Coyle (1966) : development touches each and every side of national life : political, social, even religious. Not everything has to be abolished, rather, the people will make a new arrangement of old and new ideas, old habits and new way of doing things old beliefs and new scientific theories." Thus, development makes changes in the old social system. Rogers and Svenning (1969) asserted, "development is a type of social change in which new ideas are introduced into a social system"...

Todaro (1977) defined development in a new light :

> Development must be conceived as a multi dimensional process involving major changes in social structures, popular attitudes and national institutions as well as the acceleration of economic growth, the reduction of inequality and the eradication of absolute poverty. Development must be tuned to the diverse basic needs and desires of individuals and social groups.

Referring to development as essentially a learning process, Ackoff (1984) is of the view :

> Development, contrary to what many believe, is not a condition or a state defined by what people have. It is a capacity defined by what they can do with whatever they have to improve their quality of life and that of others. Therefore, development is more possession of a desire for improvement and knowledge than it is of wealth.

Fulfilment of the basic needs of the people of a country is essential not only for economic reasons but also for psychological reasons. According to Goulet (1971), there are three components of development : life sustenance, self-esteem and freedom. All these three components are equally important no doubt the first i. e. life sustenance is fundamental one: Without the means of fulfilling primary needs such as food, clothing, shelter, health, education and employment, no human being can have self-esteem. To a person who is poor and has no self-esteem; freedom will have no meaning.

Thus, development should mean identification of sectors of population which need help the most, and working toward the fulfilment of their basic needs. It should mean reorganization of society in order to produce goods and services required to meet those demands. For reaching these goals, administrative and structural changes are essential. Otherwise, the quality of life will improve only for certain sections of society that are already in a better position while taking into account the concept of development as defined differently by different people, we can say : it broadly entails and suggests a process of change that is multidimensional social, economic, political and cultural. It also entails a change in their structures and attitudes. The change ought to create a more culturally homogeneous and consesual society endeavouring to enhance economic progress and capability so that the basic economic needs like food, shelter, clothing, education, health can be fulfilled. Development also entails the creation of streamlines and processes for the participation of groups and individuals in whole process of contemplated change so that they become an integral part of whole process and their consent is assumed to have been taken into account. Development, therefore, can be said to be an all embracing concept encompassing economic, social, cultural, educational and political aspects of the society. It is the sum total of all-round balanced and planned growth.

Generally speaking national development must, therefore, focus on mobilizing human potential through : (a) access to material resources like good health, education, housing and food, (b) creation of a culture and environment that guarantees freedom, human rights and personal self-respect.

National development implies the structure and cultural aspects of change and transformation but it also implies a certain concretization of factors and indicators for different countries. It, therefore, means to identify a stage at which the changes in different aspects of society, economy and polity complement each other so that the process of national development can continue smoothly.

Media Policy and Five Year Plans

In the First Five Year Plan (1950-56) it was recognized that all available methods of communication will have to be developed and the people approached through the written and spoken word, no less than through radio, film song and drama. Above all, steps will have to be taken to provide literature and information for the people in simple language and on a scale equal to the needs of the country.

The Second Five Year document (1956-61) stressed that "the plan has to be carried into every home in the language and the symbol of the people and expressed in terms of their common needs and problems". It also outlined the measures for expansion of plan publicity through the mass media of communication.

Intensifying the existing arrangements for bringing home the implications of rapid development and carrying the message of the plan to the masses throughout the country was proposed in the Third Five Year

Plan (1961-66). The subsequent plan documents also emphasised different aspects of communication strategy for development.

The Fourth Plan (1969-74) felt the need to inform the people in the rural areas and particularly those in backward regions, about the specific schemes in agriculture, forestry, road construction, marketing, the supply of credit and other inputs so that the benefits of these programmes are more widely stressed.

Expansion of television network to provide much needed support to education and to promote social and economic development was stressed in the Fifth Five Year Plan (1974-79). For this purpose the SITE (August 1, 1975 to July 31, 1976) was introduced in the six states. It was for the first time that an effort was made at a heavy investment to bring the message of modernisation to the rural folks. The SITE objectives included the testing of the value of satellite technology in the rapid development of effective mass communication in developing countries.

From the Sixth Plan (1980-85) onwards, fund allocation for electronic media and particularly television progressively increased which led to massive expansion of television.

The objectives of the media policy in the Seventh Five Year Plan (1985-90) were : (i) national and emotional integration of various regions of the country; (ii) utilisation of the medium as a means of development and social uplift; and (iii) dissemination of information and entertainment.

The plan envisaged the objective of TV reaching the remotest parts of the country through a three-tier service : primary service, national service and local service. The major thrust of the seventh plan relating to information and broadcasting sector was on raising the level of consciousness of the people. It laid emphasis on skilful synthesis of traditional and folk forms of communication on one hand and modern audio-visual media including satellite communication on the other.

Keeping in view the above objectives, the thrust of Doordarshan in the previous two decades and especially the thrust of Eighth Five Year Plan (1992-97) has also been to consolidate the achievements of earlier plans by suitably augmenting the production facilities at the existing centres and replacing equipment which has outlived its useful life, extension of coverage to about 76 per cent of the population and in raising the use of satellite linkage. During the Eighth Plan, the existing satellite based services have been emphasized to be expanded with main emphasis on introduction of more regional services in the languages of the state through terrestrial rebroadcast transmitters. The Eighth Plan, therefore, visualies an unprecedented growth in terms of extension of coverage, satellite services, software schemes and production facilities. Even in the earlier Five Year Plans the role of media has been greatly emphasized, to provide communication support and inform the general masses about the objectives, targets and benefits of the plans.

The government later on introduced the Prasar Bharati Act 1990 in September 1990. However, the continued foot dragging on the implementation of the Prasar Bharati Act and the yawning gap between the government's rhetoric and its practice, clearly shows that autonomy for the electronic media is as distant a dream as ever. The Vardan Committee was also set up by the government for the regulation of satellite and cable TV. Consequently the government introduced The Cable Television Networks (Regulation) Bill, 1993 in the Rajya Sabha on August 8, 1993 and passed it on December 13 in the same year. The Bill got parliamentary approval on March 14, 1994 when it was passed by Lok Sabha. The Bill aims at regulating the operation of cable television networks in the entire country so as to bring uniformity in their operation. The vast potential of new technology is intended to be utilised for the dissemination of information and entertainment. It has been clearly recognised in the Bill that there has been a haphazard mushrooming of cable television networks all over the country during the last few years as a result of the availability of signals of foreign television networks via satellites. This has been perceived as a cultural invasion in many quarters since the programmes once available on their satellite channels are predominantly western and totally alien to our culture and way of life. The Information and Broadcasting Minister, while passing the Bill said that the Bill was only the first step towards regulating the working of cable networks and the ministry would also take into account the Supreme Court verdict on regulating air waves.

The International Commission for the Study of Communication Problems (1977) popularly known as MacBride Commission was established by UNESCO to study, among other issues, such as increasing importance attached to communication as a social phenomenon and the consequent interest shown in the development of communication media, the growing impact and repercussions of technological progress in the field etc. Some of the important recommendations of the Commission are :

— Communication be no longer regarded merely as an incidental service and its development left to chance. Recognition of its potential warrants the formulation by all nations, and particularly developing countries, of comprehensive communication policies linked to overall social, cultural, economic and political goals.

Such policies should be based on inter-ministerial and inter-disciplinary consultations with broad public participation.

— Within the frame work of national development policies, each country will have to work out its own set of priorities bearing in mind that it will not be possible to move in all directions at the same time.

— Development strategies should incorporate communication policies as an integral part in the diagnosis of needs and in the design and implementation of selected priorities. In this respect communication should be considered a major development resource, a vehicle to ensure real political participation in decision making, a central information base for defining policy options, and an instrument for creating awareness of national priorities.

The national government, under Jawaharlal Nehru visualised broadcasting as a public service. Since then, the motto of the official Indian media has been to inform, to educate, and to entertain the people. Thus, any other foreign medium, which fell short of this expectation, was scrupulously debarred from making its presence felt in India. But in this new age of glastnost, India cannot have a cocoon like existence. In her eagerness to keep pace with time, India 'opened' her economy to the multinational companies and her society to the foreign electronic media. The foreign media seized the opportunity and entered the Indian society with a bang. Under such circumstances the role of media policy can be suspected.

There has been phenomenal expansion of mass media structures in the country since independence, and more so during the last two decades. Apart from the traditional mass media, print media and the radio—the advent of television and subsequently satellite television, video and now foreign satellite channels through cable television has completely changed the media scenario in the country as never before. Unwittingly the established media policy of India now stands reversed i. e., to entertain, to inform, to educate and to instruct foreign electronic media have heralded the era of information in India. We are over loaded with information. In other words we are soon passing from the age of information into the age of communication noise. These foreign channels now seem determined to teach the art and craft of consumerism to the Indians at large. The advertisement blitz made by these channels will soon create a society purely driven by 'market forces'. This will bring about the distortion of the value orientations of the Indian society. The foreign electronic media also exert an indirect influence on us by influencing the very behaviour of our own media. Thus, either in their effort to be in the race, or in their eagerness to learn from their foreign big brothers in the field, the domestic electronic media, too, will only reinforce the overall design of the foreign electronic media on India. All these new found realities in the Indian media scenario are sure to falsify what Mahatma Gandhi had said : "I want the cultures of all lands to blow as freely as possible in India. But I refuse to be swept off my feet by any of them." Now, this pious wish of the Mahatma Gandhi stands shattered by the invasion of the foreign electronic media. Under present circumstances what shape can be given to the Indian media policy for the socio-economic development of the country which may also fulfil the dreams of Gandhiji.

Yadava (1994) is of the view that despite the limited access and the urban bias, mass media have been effective in communicating hard news, significant political issues and relevant development information. Vikram Sarabhai (1991) had also felt that in any developing country, one of the prime ingredients of development is the dissemination of information about new fertilizers, seeds, insecticides, cropping patterns, new goods and services, new living patterns, etc. Therefore, television is the ideal medium to convey information and news to the people, particularly to the illiterate segment of population, on whom such an audio-visual medium, would have profound impact.

The role of television in the various spheres cannot be undermined. In this context Srivastava (1992) revealed that majority of the viewers did find television programmes useful in inducing changes in the prevailing set-up of the society. They also felt that the TV programmes help them in analyzing the process of change going on in society from different angles. Saksena (1988) reported that television has contributed a great deal to the information explosion. It has provided to the people a window on the social and cultural milieu in other parts of the country. Thus, Doordarshan has played a vital role in promoting unity and national integration.

Suggestions

No media policy can succeed without defining political and economic goals explicitly and implicitly. Democratic planning under a parliamentary domocracy has been defined as "democratic persuasion to bring about the participation and co-operation of all; democratic planning involving all groups from the villages to the National Government at all levels and the use and strengthening of democratic institutions to administer and speed development.

Policy Perspective : Emerging Issues

The first and foremost objective of India's media policy should be to preserve and strengthen the democratic way of life. Mass communication efforts should be directed at inculcating an abiding faith among the people in democratic institutions such as free and fair elections, rule of law, independence of judiciary, freedom of press, secular character of state, etc.

The policy should also promote understanding and involvement of people in the socio-economic changes and developmental activities taking place in the country. The media thus, should quicken the process of development.

Media policy should be directed toward the provision of those goods and services which meet basic needs and the yardstick for measuring the degrees and effectiveness of development should be some index of the extent to which basic needs are fulfilled e. g. indicators of infant mortality, life expectancy and basic literacy have been used as the components of a composite Physical Quality of Life Index (PQLI) that is designed to measure results in the meeting of basic needs, rather than inputs such as income (Morris, 1979).

— Any policy of culture and communication should be built within a paradigm which is both holistic and integrative, so as to combine the local reality, people's perception and needs and desired aspects of change.

— Media strategies for rural development will have to be essentially geared to the ethos and relevance to the people whom development plans are intended to benefit. The basis of media strategies should highlight the localness of approach and dissemination of culturally appropriate and user friendly technology. The media strategies would succeed in creating the right kind of climate and environment of development only, within the parameters and constraints, which are associated with the rural population. These strategies would have to be innovative, realistic and shaped to the aspiration of the people specifically inhabiting rural and remote areas.

— Therefore, the media policy is needed especially in the present day context of growing exasperating rural situations. There is a need to divert the media with the specific focus on rural sector and its communication through local dialect.

The new communication technologies increase the inequalities between the information rich and the information poor in a system. According to Rogers (1986) as new communication technologies appear on the market in an increasingly rapid sequence, the overall degree of information inequality in a society may increase. Undoubtedly, new communication technologies are relatively expensive, it is only the socio-economic elite who can afford these new media. The widening of information gap will continue unless strategies are explicitly followed to prevent it. Hence, media planners will have to be very careful while devising the rules and regulations for new information technologies for the proper development of the country.

To the end, the greater the autonomy of the media system, the greater will be its tendency to generate balanced political information contents (in ways which both reflect and protect its autonomous status). It will consequently perform primarily "moderator" and "watch dog" functions which will tend to activate "liberal citizen" and "monitor" role orientations among its audience.

REFERENCES

A Doordarshan Study (1993). New Delhi : Audience Research Unit.

Aggarwal, Vir Bala, (1992). Mass Media in Rural Development : Some Research Issues. *Communicator*, December, pp. 14-15.

Akash Bharati : National Broadcast Trust Vol. 1 (1978). Report of the Working Group on Software for Doordarshan. New Delhi : Publication Division. pp. 116-121.

An Indian Personality for Television (1985). Report of the Working Group on Software for Doordarshan. New Delhi : Publications Division. pp. 124-144.

Chatterji, P. C. (1993). Broadcasting in India. New Delhi : National Book Trust.

Chawla, Prabhu (1989). Doordarshan Hijacking the Medium. *India Today*, 15 July. pp. 26-34.

Chopra Pran (1986). National Media Policy. *Media Monitor*. September-October. pp. 10-11.

Eighth Five Year Plan (1992-97). New Delhi : Planning Commission, Government of India.

Fifth Five Year Plan (1975-80). New Delhi : Planning Commission, Government of India.

First Five Year Plan (1950-51). New Delhi : Planning Commission, Government of India.

Fourth Five Year Plan (1969-74). New Delhi : Planning Commission, Government of India.

Joshi P. C. (1986). Communication and Nation Building : Perspective and Policy. *Sardar Patel Memorial Lectures (1985)*. New Delhi : Publication Division.

Kothari (1993). *The Pioneer*, 11 December.

Ministry of Information and Broadcasting (1993-94). Annual Report. New Delhi : Publications Division, Govt. of India.

Second Five Year Plan (1956-61). New Delhi : Planning Commission, Government of India.

Seventh Five Year Plan (1985-90). New Delhi : Planning Commission, Government of India.

Sixth Five Year Plan (1980-85). New Delhi : Planning Commission, Government of India.

Srivastava, U.K. (1987). National Cost of Television in India in the year 2000 : Socio-economic and Political Implications and Issues. *Media Asia 14* (3) : 136-148.

The Cable Television Networks (Regulation) Bill 1993.

UNESCO (1980). Many Voices One World. The International Commission for the Study of Communication Problems. pp. 40-41.

Vardan Committee (1992). Summary of the Report. *Communicator* XXVII (I) : 14-17.

Vikram Sarabhai (1991). Mass Media and Development. In : *Government Media : Autonomy and After* (Ed.), G. S. Bhargavan. New Delhi : Concept Publishing Company.

Vir Bala and Kulwinder Singh, (1992). Communication Strategies for Rural Development. *Vidura*. pp. 39-41.

Yadava, J. S. (1994). Communication and Development : The Indian Experience. In : *Media and Development*, M. R. Dua and V. S. Gupta (eds.). New Delhi : Har Anand Publications.

8

ENVIRONMENT, DEVELOPMENT AND WOMEN'S ISSUES

C. Jayanthi

It is a well known fact that women are most affected by drastic changes in environment, be it scarcity of water, fuel or poverty. In Indian villages, lack of proper drinking water increases women's burden as they have to walk the extra mile in search of water. Similar is the case with fuel. As trees are cut down and forests recede, women have to walk a longer distance to fetch fuel for their household use. All this is of course linked to poverty as the burden of living on a poor, unskilled woman is much more severe. It has in fact led to the coinage of the term "feminisation of poverty".

Of the world's 1.2 billion poor, almost 70 per cent are estimated to be women, according to UN statistics. Of about 400 million poor in India, women face a similar situation. If poverty is defined as the "inability to attain a minimal standard of living" then women more than men are likely to fall into this category due to their lower status. As women's education has over centuries taken less priority than men's, they acquired lesser skills, have lesser access to resources and property than men. With the result that it drives them into low-income occupations in which they are economically exploited. They also frequently migrate from their homes across international borders where they are hired as domestic servants at the risk of economic and sexual exploitation.

The Jakarta declaration for the advancement of women in Asia and the Pacific, outcome of the second UN Asian and Pacific ministerial conference on women in development, last year, says : Women, in particular, those who are elderly, disabled and from indigenous and minority cultures, suffer the most under conditions of absolute poverty.

The number of rural and urban slum women living in poverty is increasing at a faster rate than for men and the proportion of women among the poor is growing.

Poverty tends to reduce women to working in informal sectors due to lack of skills with practically no legislative protection and trade union support. This is true of a vast majority of women in India who are engaged in rural areas in subsistence agriculture and as migrant domestic and construction site workers residing in urban slums.

One of the major reasons for the increased participation of women is indirectly due to the development of vast urban centres in the country—the migration of men to urban areas in search of work which requires more skills. There is also the continued lack of recognition in certain pockets of the country of women's contribution to agriculture due to the cultural "veil" that persists and devalues women's unpaid activity. The more cheerful side of the coin is that the government has announced and got underway a few schemes for fuller and productive participation of women in agriculture. If we were to look at the 1991 census, 78 per cent of women workers form a third of total agricultural force as a large majority of them are primarily dependent on agriculture for a livelihood.

According to a paper presented on "Women and agricultural work" at the British Council seminar sometime ago and which is indeed a reality in the rural areas, "Although almost all rural women are involved to different degrees in agriculture, the nature and extent of their involvement varies widely across regions and is strongly influenced by a nexus of class/caste hierarchy in rural India with 'inside' work in the domestic sphere denoting higher status than 'outside' work as field workers." Apart from gender distinctions based on caste hierarchy which accords lower status to women field workers, there are distinctions based on crop cultivation as well as regions. So, as the paper points out, the gender divisions of tasks is sequential with women being preferred for certain activities such as transplanting, weeding, harvesting and specific post-harvesting operations.

Punjab, Haryana and UP have low female participation in agriculture, whereas in Rajasthan and Himachal Pradesh, where subsistence agriculture is practised, the reverse is the case. There is also the fact that in the former three states, resorting to wage work among female cultivators is considered "a social disgrace". In the North-East, female participation is almost 45 per cent. In Gujarat, Madhya Pradesh and Maharashtra, the high female participation rate is related to commercial crops and high male migration to urban areas.

According to the Annual Report 1994-95 of the Ministry of Agriculture, several schemes have been implemented with a view to including "women farmers and to recognise them as clientele of all agricultural support services". The states include Karnataka, Tamil Nadu, Orissa and Madhya Pradesh with Danish assistance and Gujarat and Andhra Pradesh with Dutch assistance. The project is being implemented in all districts except Bidar with a total cost of Rs. 1,25,400,000. The project has been extended to be trained under the scheme in new technologies. Until June 1994, 14,328 women were trained. It is to heartening to see beginnings being made so that women acquire skills and survive better.

According to a recent book by Poonam Smith-Sreen, *Accountability in Development Organisations*, "...Female (work) participation rates are highly correlated to poverty and landlessness in rural India, women go to work when the household incomes do not suffice their basic needs; women workers are paid less than men for the same operations and in some industries like *bidi*-making and *chikan* where women are 90 per cent of the workers, they are exploited by the middlemen."

Although the impact of the structural adjustment policies on women in India is yet to be established, in Tanzania where it was hastily implemented, it led to the collapse of the local textile industry due to imports from Pakistan and women workers were the first to go alongwith the displacement of jobs. So, it goes without saying that poverty accords women lower status in life and lifelong situation of economic and social exploitation out of which few escape due to lack of access to resources and skills.

Apart from poverty the environmental ravages that women suffer from are mostly armed conflicts. Wartime atrocities against women have been the maximum during current times, be it the Gulf war, the war in Afghanistan or the Bosnian war. Women and children have been the worst victims of war, even though they are never the perpetrators of it. Amnesty International's recent report on the effect of the Afghanistan war over the past three years on the lives of women and children which have been devastated reads like a horror story.

The Report reveals that the various political factions have specifically aimed at residential areas since they have been fighting for territory as of April 1992. Says the report, "Armed groups have massacred defenceless women in their homes or have brutally beaten and raped them. Scores of young women have been abducted and then raped, taken as wives by commanders or sold into prostitution. Some have committed suicide to avoid such a fate. Scores of women have reportedly 'disappeared' and several have been stoned to death. Hundreds of thousands of women and children have fled their homes in terror only to suffer further abuses during their flight or in refugee camps. Many are traumatised by the horrific abuses they have suffered or witnessed." India as well as other neighbouring countries have been an influx of Afghani refugees over the past few years. The Amnesty report points out that the Mujahideen groups which establish control over a pocket of territory, subject the entire local populace to violence. "The conquerors often celebrate by killing and raping women and looting property. Alongside these apalling abuses, women have been prevented from exercising some of their fundamental rights—including the rights to association, freedom of expression and employment—Mujahideen groups which consider such activities to be un-Islamic for women."

In a book brought out by Panos, *Arms to Protect*, an Indian woman equates her experience of the 1947 Indo-Pak partition violence to the Bosnian war. She says, "There was so much fear, in July 1947... People talk of Bosnia, but partition was the first large scale migration in the name of religion. Everyone blamed the British. Muslims became their tool. It is the fault of our people (Hindus) too... It is the same from ancient history. All the invadors always understood women to be a commodity, not human beings... Men just thought that women are a thing of beauty or a thing to breed children." Things do not seem to have changed drastically since then. In December 1993, the UN General Assembly adopted the declaration on the "Elimination of violence against women". Article one of the Declaration defines violence against women as : Any act of gender-based violence that results in physical, sexual, psychological harm or suffering to women, including threats of such acts, coercion or arbitrary deprivation of liberty, whether occurring in public or private life. Despite existence of laws, inadequate implementation by authorities leads to the perpetuation of violence against women. In India, we have the Dowry Prohibition Act, Prevention of Immoral Traffic Act and Indecent Representation of Women Act, to name a few. However, this has hardly stopped anyone from committing crimes with impunity. Law enforcement agencies, human rights groups and women's organisations can be mobilised for effective implementation of laws spreading awareness of gender-based violence.

The first NCW Annual Report for the year 1992-93 has said that although the Dowry Prohibition Act, 1961 was a special law, offences covered by it were not treated as committed against the State but against the individual woman, contributing to its inefficacy. It has pointed out that many of the states did not have a special agency to detect and investigate offences under the Act, which itself treated offences as cognizable for certain limited purposes. The dowry legislation has strangely strengthened resistance among families against giving girls their share in patrimonial property. It points out that, "In spite of the equal rights given in the parental property, the parents are still reluctant to give an equal share in their property to the girls and also justify the same by saying that they cannot give fat dowries to sons-in-law and also give an equal share in the property to the daughters. It is becoming a vicious circle and the sufferer is the girl since the dowry is taken away by the husband and husband's family and she is in no way benefited by it. At the same time, if gifts by the parents, relatives or friends at the time of the marriage are totally banned, the girl would be left penniless." The reason why the Dowry Prohibition Act was amended in the recent past to allow gifts which may be given to the girl with a safeguard that all of them should be listed, stating that the commission proposed that such gifts be registered.

Measures are required, especially so, in the developing world where economic inequities have more often than not had their fallout in gender disparities, to improve a woman's environment and thereby her ability to earn income, achieve economic self-reliance, inherit, own and dispose off property and have access to credit.

The Indian Government has made a few in roads in the area of making credit available to poor urban and rural women. The two programmes MSY and RMK were started by the Department of Women and Child Development in late 1993. The former functions through a network of post offices in rural areas with the aim of encouraging thrift among rural women so that they could start savings and be assured of a security deposit. For an amount of upto Rs. 300 kept in the post office for a "lock-in period" of one year, the government gives an incentive of 25 per cent, which means an account holder who has deposited Rs. 3,000 will get Rs. 375 at the end of the year.

The RMK is a national credit fund for poor rural and urban women, run with the help of NGOs and SHGs. Loans for short term purposes upto Rs. 2,500 and for medium purposes of upto Rs. 5,000 per borrower are supported by RMK. Several State schemes have also been launched. All this, however, remains a drop in the ocean, as the magnitude of the problem is fairly large. Shrouded in a culture of silence, whether poor or middle class, and handicapped by economic hardships and dependencies, women find it difficult to assert themselves for their rights.

According to an ILO publication on, Employment and Population, 1994, "Remunerated employment in general is a factor which contributes in varying degrees to changing social and economic relationships within households, both in developed and developing countries... The impact of female employment on fertility has been increasing steadily throughout the developed countries, especially since World War II. In developed countries, average fertility fell below replacement level in the early 1970s, and has continued to fall since then. During the same period, there were increases in female employment. Population specialists explain this negative association as being partly due to the rising opportunity cost of child-bearing and child care. Today female employment is regarded as an important determinant of fertility in developed countries."

However, women who do not join the workforce make a substantial contribution to the household economy which is not accounted for even while computing labour statistics. They are not paid for it, they are not acknowledged for it. So, women's work unless it is in the formal wage sector is ignored.

According to the Human Development Report 1995, brought out by the UNDP, "The idea should be resisted that, to be valued, human activity must always be assigned a market price. Many of the things that make life worth living carry no price. We do not advocate that all activities within a family or a community must be monetised to be given adequate recognition. Most of the activities have a value that extends far beyond any economic valuation. Yet, we face the dilemma that not giving an economic valuation to these activities risks seriously underestimating the contribution of women. There is no adequate reward or recognition for the burden of work that women carry... If these unpaid activities were treated as market transactions at the prevailing wages, they would yield huge monetary valuations—a staggering $ 16 trillion or about 70 per cent more than the officially estimated $ 23 trillion of the global output. Of this $16 trillion, $ 11 trillion is the non-monetised, "invisible" contribution of women."

So, it goes without saying that the silence of women and the acceptance of their fate as sacrificial goals works marvellously well for established patriarchal set-ups. The only weapon to fight this with is education as it brings in self-awareness, increases self-worth and allows women to seek self-fulfilment in areas other than child-bearing and rearing.

9

MEDIA—INDIA 2000

Prem Kumar

It is a favourite pastime of Indian journalists to make predictions, particularly about what they describe as politics. The predictions often go wrong giving them an opportunity to analyse the surprise results. Now, making predictions is an old skill of this country based on certain logic. Neither Indian politics nor most journalism here has much of logic and predictions would naturally come untrue. I will not even try to predict anything about journalism five years hence. I will only share with you some impressions, some hunches based on the current trends and on the nature of people who are running the show and on the requirement of people who are supposed to be catered to.

First about the people, the common men, the readers or listeners or viewers of the media. We live in the world of democracy which is said to be for the people, of the people and by the people, etc. The fact is that the common man is the last priority in this country in the matter of politics, administration, education, social welfare and even media attention. We dish out irrelevant, at times silly stuff under the excuse that the people want it—and we decide about what they want sitting in our armed chairs in air-conditioned offices. The people are getting aware, even restive over the situation. They will make greater demands on media in days to come. They will dictate their choices. The media will have to give in to their wishes. The media in India have yet to know and assess what the people want. They will be trying to find out in the next five years and what they find will influence their effort in the year 2000.

Among the most important things that the common man will want is that he wants to occupy centre-stage, denied to him for long by the VIPs and VVIPs. The concept of essential elements of news will undergo a change as for as the word prominence is concerned. He is the prominent person in today's world and he wants more written about himself. The media will have to cover more and more of him. We will see more of the man in the street, of course the woman too, covered or uncovered by the media.

Without going into greater detail, I feel that the people will demand of the media, greater credibility, accuracy, objectivity, detail, keener observation, more interesting description and narration, more scientific analysis, investigation and interpretation. More of these elements are bound to be seen in future.

Apart from what the people want them to do, the media will undergo a certain amount of change out of compulsion. The world is changing fast and those in this country, though slow to react and slow to change will have to fall in line particularly because the commercial requirement will influence them. There is and will be more fierce competition domestically and globally, among the media of the print type and among the electronic media and among these two. The salesmanship is dominating all the fields of human activity and it is going to take its toll in the world of media too. Technology is getting updated fast and is influencing all activities. Media effort will be affected by it. There are two processes on at the same time. The small is being expanded and developed vertically and horizontally for greater reach, higher profits and just for the love of expansion. The media units will expand in the process. There are already indications in the chains of newspapers and TV systems of such a trend. Privatisation will take over most part of electronic media and liberalisation will affect both the electronic and print media in the days to come. While the existing chains will expand, there will be many more small and new entrepreneurs to come on the scene and try their luck in the new gold rush in the media field. It will not be a surprise if journalists themselves who have been depending on salaried jobs in the past themselves become entrepreneurs. This will bring in some professionalism and such a trend is already visible though in a small way at present.

There is going to be a lot of decentralisation in the media world. More regional and local papers, more specialised journals, more small radio and TV networks to cater to the local needs, larger regional language papers and journals. An important factor in this process will be a big boost to the economic journalism both in the print and electronic media. The signs are already there for everyone to see. It is felt that the common man, for once is getting a lot interested in economic matters and may, in the years to come, let this interest overtake the political interest. The media will take note of this and cater to his needs. Incidentally, the dominant role of politics, or what the mediamen perceive to be politics, is very slow to go from the Indian media scene. This to me is a losing game and will not go on for ever. Subjects other than politics will have to be given their due place in the media scene and not by way of an apology to compensate for the dominant political input. Not enough is being done at present to cover these subjects, development for instance.

As for as the content of the media coverage is concerned, one can safely say that there is still a lot of scope to inject human interest element in the effort. It is to the minimum at present. In fact, many of our colleagues have yet to realise its importance and scope. Those who do find it difficult to pay it enough attention and time. There are certain flashes but it has yet to become an integral part of media output. This is one reason why an average reader spends only a few minutes going through the daily newspaper, or concentrates on pictures in magazines, or devotes much of the time on films and film based programmes on TV. It is sad, hopeful, the situation will change in the next five years. There will be more and more of human interest stuff in papers and on TV.

It is also important to mention investigative and interpretative journalism while talking about the content. These two types of writing have been introduced to this country's media world and there are some shining examples of this effort by some veteran and not so veteran mediamen. Unfortunately, there is also a lot of fake stuff dished out in the name investigation. There are plants and leaks which are entertained too often and presented as an investigative effort. This, it is quite likely, will change and more scientific and systematic effort will be made to tackle this department of media activity. More resources have to go into it, more proper manpower will be required for it and more effective methods and systems developed for the purpose. It is likely to be so in the next few years. The main reason is that the people would not be satisfied with anything less. The same is true of interpretative writing or telecasting. We are great ones when it comes to commenting and offering opinions and interpretation gets mixed up with opinion. In fact much of interpretation is comment. There are certain rules of the game and they have got to be followed if a proper interpretation is to be done. It will have to be done as the people in future may not like to be confused as much as at present by the mediamen. They will want to be clear about what is happening and why it is happening.

A word about development coverage should be in order. Many people have wrong notions about it. For them, it means praise for what is done in the field. Those who like to use a more subtle word want it to be positive or constructive. Development journalism in the real sense is yet to come in the Indian media. More and more persons, better qualified and trained, will have to be engaged in this task and more space and time will have to be given to it. Perhaps it will partially be achieved in the next few years.

Apart from content, a lot of stress is being laid on presentation of the media content. The more enthusiastic among the media persons and their masters are talking about media products and the packaging. It is a matter of a separate debate as far as its merits and demerits are concerned but one thing is obvious. More and more resources and human effort will go into this department and there will be a keen competition on making the presentation more and more attractive. More visuals, all types of them, are the in-thing. More colour, greater variety in text presentation, more stress on lay-out will be there. It is alright as long as these elements make the people read or view the output.

As one talks of presentation, one has to mention technology which is making the competition keener. It is all becoming a hightech affair. The typography and printing is getting more sophisticated every day. The TV production and transmission is also depending on the latest technology. As the technology is getting updated fast, the media world will reflect the changes in the days to come. One is not even very sure what is in store for him in the next five years. Computers, anyway, have been introduced widely and they would have literally taken over by the year 2000.

While technology will take care of itself, the more important thing for the Indian media is to pay more attention to education and training of human part of the setup. Whatever is being done at present is very inadequate, at times even irrelevant. Those in the field of média education should seriously think about this problem and come up with a really efficient and effective, relevant and useful, education programme to cope with the needs of the media in the next few years.

10

ETHICS, VALUES AND MEDIA

Sunil Saxena

I would like to look at this issue at two different levels. The first is the issue of ethics as seen within and outside the media and how it is affecting the media's credibility; and the second is the change in values that the media, especially the audio-visual media, has brought about.

Both are critical issues, and have become subject of increased debate among media practitioners and media educators. There is also a growing difference in perception between the readers and viewers on the question of what is ethical and what is unethical when it comes to reporting events. This is evident from the growing refrain among readers about the credibility of the media. The trust and confidence which the Indian media once enjoyed is getting eroded in the public eye.

This is not to say that people have lost faith in Indian media altogether. On the contrary, people believe what the journalists say. There is definitely more confidence in print media reports than in government-sponsored bulletins. But there are also nagging doubts that journalists are not reporting facts accurately; that they are hedging on issues; that they are more prone to cover reports aimed to attract a wider readership base than to contribute to social good.

There is also a feeling that the media gives one side of the picture only; that it does not do justice to the individual or institution whose image has been tarnished; that the media suffers from a mob mentality when it comes to dealing with sensitive issues.

It will be wrong to brush away these complaints as unjustified, and the readers impressions as baseless. There is certainly an element of truth in them. Even newsmen recognise this. A common refrain in newsrooms is that more and more reporters are resorting to the practice of convincing generalities. They don't always name sources; instead they hide behind such generalities as sources confirm or according to sources close to the prime minister. Such a tendency can be justified when the stories are of a sensitive nature and the reporter wants to protect the identity of the source. But unfortunately this is not always the case. Very often an impeccable source is used to tell a whole story, making the readers wonder whether the impeccable source is the reporter himself or a figment of his imagination.

Tougher Gatekeeping Needed

Another problem is that the reporters don't limit themselves to facts; instead they let their opinion about individuals or institutions creep into their stories. Mostly, such assessments or valuations are personal. How many times we read of controversial officials or tainted politicians without learning why the official is controversial or politician tainted. Surely, this cannot enhance media credibility. A much tougher gatekeeping is needed.

Another abused ethical question is the right of reply. Aggrieved parties are often not given the chance to state their case. Even when their version does appear it has been abridged in the interest of good editing. I don't wish to contest the editor's right to publish what he thinks is appropriate. This right is absolute and must rest with the editor. But what needs to be examined is how balanced are the reports being published in Indian newspapers. There certainly has been an awakening on this issue. But it is not enough. Repeated surveys have shown that either the aggrieved party is not given a fair chance to present his point of view or else what he says has been shortened to such an extent that the impact is lost. This is clearly unfair and needs to be redressed.

The credibility of newspaper is also being affected by reports of journalists taking sides on account of personal, financial or ideological reasons. There is now enough evidence to believe that journalists subscribing to extreme right or extreme left views have entered the profession, and are peddling points of views that are in keeping with the needs of their ideological mentors. This is an unfortunate development, and holds grave implications about the integrity of the Indian media. There is nothing wrong in giving all the points of view and letting the reader make up his mind; but when this exercise is carried out to achieve certain political or ideological ends then it needs to be viewed with great suspicion.

There is also a need to look into financial inducements that are offered to newsmen by political parties and companies. The small fortunes paid by Mr. Mulayam Singh Yadav to newsmen in Uttar Pradesh indicate how deep this malaise has spread. Sums amounting from 10 to 15 lakhs were disbursed by Mr. Mulayam Singh to turn the press pliant.

Similarly, a fiscal ceiling needs to be arrived at regarding the gifts that companies disburse to newsmen. Should they be limited to calendars or diaries? Or should they include products like watches or suitlengths? How far can one go in accepting such freebies—a free trip, a free lunch. Or may be more? This is a grave ethical question again, and needs to be attended to if doubts have to be removed from people's minds regarding the integrity of the media.

The right to privacy fortunately is not a major issue as far as the Indian press is concerned. We, in India, are still not obsessed with the private lives of officials or politicians; nor do we badger victims of crime or their families to the breaking point. But this is an area that must be kept in mind. Privacy of individuals must be respected.

At the second level I wish to examine the impact of the audio-visual media on our values. Since the launch of the Star TV on May 15, 1991 and the arrival of several desi television channels on the small screen the Indian mindset and thinking has undergone a revolution. The living room has become an area of cultural conflict; and the idiot box the stimuli that has led to a crumbling of social norms and mores.

The days of insularity are over. Television is producing new role models, generating new concepts about lifestyle, fashion and behaviour. Cultural barriers are crumbling. The divide between the cultural haves and have-nots is becoming deeper, breeding deep social conflicts.

There is little doubt that the TV waves are buffeting the young mind, and by extension the prevailing standards in the society. It is now established that there is a drop in metabolic rate among children watching favourite TV programmes with rapt attention. They go into a trance-like state, and the result can roughly be compared to that of post-hypnotic suggestion. This means that several strong messages are going straight into the unconscious mind, influencing thinking patterns. The pity is that neither the child nor the parents are aware of the strength or nature of messages that have been imbibed.

This is a dangerous situation. Such messages may implode with worrisome implications, leading to momentary loss of reason or rationality. There is the additional danger of a child's physical growth being affected too, because he is busy watching television when he should be playing. Already there is sharp fall in time spent with other children, and on books.

Children are now maturing quickly and want to move on to Mills and Boon titles instead of spending time on comics and children's books. The result is that a child stops behaving like a child and starts emulating the adults or hankers after an adult lifestyle even before he is ready for it.

On the child and teenager's agenda too are soap operas and serials like *The Bold and the Beautiful* and *Santa Barbara*. Even the desi soaps from *Junoon* to *Shanti* are patterned on western soaps reflecting a lifestyle that is not rooted in reality. These serials thrive on violence, sex and feuds, causing a conflict. Can we sustain it? Can our existing social mores of rational behaviour absorb it? Already there is an increase in permissive-ness in society; pre-marital sex is on the rise.

The conflict is not limited to the cultural plane alone. It also has financial implications. There is a new boom in spending; profligacy is on the rise, thanks to the rising affluence of the middle class. This is bound to create more social barriers between the rich and the poor. Frustration, when demands are not met, will also make its anger felt in physical or verbal outbursts, both within and without the home.

As a result of these changes, the value system is getting debased. We can't blame the satellite television alone for the changes. Liberalisation, growth of middle class, increased purchasing power, the breakdown of joint families and emergence of nuclear families and now families where both husband and wife are working are also responsible for the changing social and cultural values.

Code of Ethics

What is desperately needed is self-discipline; the need to look inwards; to set up a code of ethics. As far as the print media is concerned, it needs to ensure that :

1. All stories, barring sensitive ones where the source's identity needs to be protected, must be based on proper attribution.
2. There must be objectivity in writing stories and no valuation must be done about individuals or institutions unless it is substantiated.
3. Any gift, whether given by an individual or an institution, must be looked upon with grave suspicion. If there is even the slightest doubt that the gift is meant to influence the report then it must be rejected. Reporters not following this rule must be punished by the editor.
4. Stories must give fair and justified space to all points of view. Contradictions and clarifications must be printed prominently.

5. There should be no bias, whether racial, sexual or regional in the stories.
6. A code of ethics needs to be formulated by the mediamen. This should be displayed in the reporters' room and on the newsdesk. Also it must be published once a year in all newspapers so that the readers know what the ethical standards to which the newspapers subscribe to.
7. The institution of ombudsman must be legalised. All newspapers must appoint an ombudsman, who can be a senior newsman or a retired judge, to look into complaints of ethical misconduct.

In the case of audio-visual medium greater care must be taken to scrutinise programmes. Programmes that are sex-based or violent must be categorised. A warning must come up before the programme advising viewers whether the programme is suitable for children, teenagers or youth. Also, those programmes that are likely to affect the healthy growth of children must be beamed later at night. If possible, separate channels must be used with the viewers knowing which channel is for children and which one is for the adults. This is also now possible with the more advanced TV sets where the adults only can access certain channels.

Satellite channel is here to stay. We must accept that we are now a wired society, and television will continue to exercise an important influence on behavioural patterns. But we need to study and monitor this influence, and raise ethical barriers as and when needed.

11

SATELLITE COMMUNICATION—EMPOWERMENT AT PANCHAYATI RAJ LEVEL

A. Sengupta

Panchayati Raj institutions developed in India in the early 1960's in the aftermath of the Balwantrai Mehta Committee Report (1957) which recommended a three tier system of "democratic decentralization". But a generation of poor, illiterate, marginalised Indians later, it had become clear that there were numerous shortcomings in the system-prolonged supersessions which were both the result and the cause of the lack of regular elections, inadequate financial and managerial resources, the inadequate representation of the weaker sections. The result—the 'hijacking" of the panchayati institutions by the rural elite, and the transformation of "Panchayati Raj institutions as agencies of the state apparatus."

The Constitution (73rd Amendment) Act, 1992, attempted to rectify the situation. The Act incorporated a set of provisions relating to Panchayats in Art. 243 of the Constitution and provided various measures for strengthening them. The most significant provision was the reservation of seats for the Scheduled Castes and Scheduled Tribes, and the ensuring of not less than one third of the seats in panchayats for women. This has made possible the genuine empowerment of the people.

At a 1994 UN conference, preparatory to the 1995 Copenhagen summit on Social Development, the Union Minister of State for External Affairs, Mr. Salman Khurshid said that "The Panchayati Raj Act just enacted (73rd Amendment) gives political power to the people, but a social dimension by way of empowerment of the people will come only when the people are organised in the context of the socio-economic programmes that are meant for their own development." It means by implication argues Ramaswamy, "that the Panchayati Raj Act (Amendment) *per se* does not empower the people." But the amendment does make possible, indeed permits for the first time, that empowerment.

"Education, techonology, and openness have complex relations to development", according to the World Bank. The context in which openness has been mentioned by the World Bank is international, but it could be applied to the insular, dispersed and illiterate but intrinsically astute village gram sabhas of the subcontinent that is India, and in the context of the opportunities the new Panchayati Raj system opens up for the people. It is the use of modern technology that can speed up the process of education—going beyond literacy and giving people the wherewithal to decide for themselves.

As the WDR 1991 says, "By improving people's ability to acquire and use information, education deepens their understanding of themselves and the world, enriches their minds by broadening their experiences, and improves the choices they make as consumers, producers, and citizens. Education strengthens their ability to meet their wants and those of their family by increasing their productivity, and their potential to achieve a higher standard of living. By improving people's confidence and their ability to create and innovate, it multiplies their opportunities for personal and social achievement."

Literacy is not quite education, but is a good proxy for any quantitative analysis. Literacy rates in India are abysmal. In 1985, it was 43 per cent, while for women, it was a mere 29 per cent. (China's, in comparison was 69 per cent overall, and female literacy was 55 per cent. Even countries poorer than India—Uganda, Nigeria, Zaire, Rwanda—have a higher literacy rate). India's overall literacy was 52.11 per cent in 1991, while female literacy was only 39.42 per cent. Of special significance is the fact that in sheer numbers the situation is worsening. In 1981, there were 301.93 million illiterates in the country; this went up to 324.04 million a decade later. While literacy improved by 8.55 per cent in the 1981-91 period, the numbers of illiterates rose by 7.31 per cent.

It is axiomatic to consider literacy to be directly and positively related to GNP. One analysis of educational statistics in relation to per capita GNP in the 1970's and the early 1980's shows that for a per capita income group of less than $ 300, the illiteracy rate was 64 per cent, for $ 300 to $ 500 it dramatically reduced to 37 per cent and for an income of over $ 5,000, it was roughly estimated to be about 2 per cent. Some highly developed countries do not anymore record illiteracy rates.

But, perhaps more important in the context of true Panchayati Raj is the national equivalent of the "theology of liberation" which Goulet and Guiterrez and other Latin American theologians advocated in the 1960's. Guiterrez, a Peruvian social activist and theologian, stated that "the term development conveys a pejorative connotation... (and) is gradually being replaced by the term liberation... there will be a true development for Latin America only through liberation from the domination by capitalist countries." This view is not quite universally held today, and the dangers of placing too much emphasis on liberation (which implies a certain insularity) has been dealt with elsewhere. But, conceptually, within India, this is the constitutionally blessed empowerment of the people, their liberation from exploitation.

From the point of view of the administration, at the stage of converting policy into action, responsiveness to the needs of the people is a cliched requirement, but that the role of bureaucracy as a change agent is crucial in the empowerment process needs constant emphasis and reiteration. The traditional bureaucracy must enable and encourage the development of the new leadership. Dayal points out that a good example of administrative reforms would be the Saemaul programme in South Korea which was implemented through, most importantly, the mass involvement of people which was achieved by short training programmes of several thousand citizens in a year and by displacing the traditional leadership while changing the power coalition of village institutions.

If Panchayati Raj in India is to succeed at least now, a special effort is called for in educating the rural masses, especially women and other "weaker" sections of society, and enabling them to genuinely participate in the grassroots level democratic process. For such a thrust, speed is of the essence in the learning—and teaching—process, far beyond the less than one per cent annual growth in literacy. What is required is the equivalent of an immersion programme, both spatially and qualitatively. And to do so, perhaps the only way is by using new technology that the country itself can offer—through the medium of satellite broadcasting for education. It is not only universal, it is inexpensive and it permits the control of quality.

The role of satellites in education is not new in India. The TV Centre of All India Radio, as it was then called, began telecasting school programmes in 1965. A 1966 suggestion of the UNESCO Panel of Consultants on Space Communications that a pilot satellite project could be taken up in India "both for testing techniques and demostrating the effectiveness of telecommunications satellites while serving the priority needs of the area through a major contribution to development", finally led to the well known SITE programme of 1975-76. The SITE programme envisaged the use of NASA's Advanced Technology Satellite—F for broadcasts for 22 minutes daily in each of four languages to children in the primary school age group in about 2400 villages spread over six clusters in some of the most backward districts of India. The six states covered were Madhya Pradesh, Orissa, Bihar, Rajasthan, Andhra Pradesh and what is now Karnataka.

The SITE project also experimented with a Limited Rebroadcast System, wherein a 1 Kw VHF transmitter was used to provide local TV broadcast. This transmission, from Pij village in Gujarat formed the local TV broadcast and developmental communications experiment called the Kheda Communications Project.

SITE was followed by STEP, during 1977-79, using a Franco-German satellite, the Symphonie-I. It provided, *inter alia*, for the testing of geostationary satellites for communications and the optimal system techniques and parameters for a future Indian domestic satellite system. APPLE satellite was, in 1981, India's first geostationary communications satellite. The first INSAT satellite was launched in 1982, and since then we have come a long way with the INSAT I and II series.

The idea of an INSAT system had been first proposed in the late 1960's. The common plank on which various concepts of the system rested was that "the potential of the satellite medium can be drawn upon for rapid expansion of TV on a nationwide basis for education, national integration and development." By 1992 some 4000 Direct to Community receivers and about 50,000 VHF community television sets had been established in India. But, as Narayanan and Ramachandran note, "The mushrooming of privately owned sets has placed the concept of community sets in the background. The problem of finding financial support as well as the difficulties inherent in maintaining the community sets has only accentuated the situation."

Nevertheless, direct broadcast service (DBS) for education has increased. We are all aware of the UGC programmes, but not many of us know of the broadcasts by the Indira Gandhi National Open University, mainly curriculum based lectures for students of the university. But till the 1990's the efforts had one significant shortcoming. In a normal classroom, the teacher receives questions and comments from the students to which he/she replies—an interactive method. The regular DBS does not permit this. Distance education through a "talkback" method, began in February 1991 with a training programme for adult education trainers.

The system consists of three major elements—the teaching end with a small studio and an uplink earth station, the receiving end, which can be a regular classroom, though in the nature of a studio to permit the talkback, and, of course, the satellite. The "live" or recorded programmes emanate as TV signals from the studio, and are uplinked to a geostationary communications satellite. The satellite receives, amplifies and retransmits these signals to any classroom within the satellite's coverage through a DRS, which is a low cost dish antenna of 8 to 12 feet diameter, the front-end receiving equipment and a television set. A talkback facility can be provided through a return voice link which can be implemented in one of two ways. Through the Public Switched Telephone Network (PSTN) a dial up long distance call can be made to the teaching end where a small EPABX can receive the calls. Otherwise, a small satellite communication terminal can be located in the classroom which transmits the processed audio signal via the satellite to the teaching end.

This much is known and to many. What is known to very few is that since 1991, there have been 24 talkback experiments, using the INSAT system, of which as many as 17 have been in 1994 and 1995. In August 1992, a talkback experiment was conducted in Bhiwani for extension education; a similar one was taken up by the Government of Gujarat in October 1994. Organisations like the UGC, IETE, IGNOU, AIMA and the SBI have collaborated with the Indian Space Research Organisation (ISRO), in experimenting with the methodology.

It is significant that this new technology has arrived in tandem with the new Panchayati Raj system, as an aid to educating the new, grassroots level leaders. During February 15-18, the Government of Karnataka, in collaboration with ISRO, conducted a pilot project for training "development functionaries" spread out in all the districts of the State, using an interactive satellite broadcasting network. The programme covered three areas—the training of village health workers, of progressive farmers and functionaries in watershed development, and, perhaps the most significant, of elected gram panchayat women members. In this regard, the preamble to the order of the Government of Karnataka states very simply "...given the relatively lower educational qualifications of women, as well as their lack of political experience, their effective participation in panchayati raj will need to be facilitated through systematic training and communication support." (Government Order No. WCD 57 SWW 94 Bangalore, dated 12.7.1994). The subsequent training of women representatives, remaining within their districts but reaching out to the best help available, is a landmark in the history of women's empowerment in India, but has gone largely unnoticed. In the midst of "Close-up Antakshari" and "Jodi Poduttham", consumerism has overtaken our media.

On February 23, 1995, the Prime Minister dedicated to the nation, a channel on the INSAT system for training and devèlopment communications. Hopefully other States will take up the opportunity that our satellite system today offers for making Panchayati Raj a genuinely participatory process. There is a major ISRO programme on the anvil for developmental efforts through a direct broadcast and talkback project in Jhabua, one of the least developed districts of the country. The project is expected to begin in May 1996, with training in adult education, panchayati raj, wasteland development and public health through approximately 150 DBS receiving centres and 12 talkback stations.

But Government cannot, perhaps should not, do all. This is clearly an area into which the non-governmental agencies must step in, as indeed the Prime Minister hoped as he dedicated the exclusive channel. Initial analyses of the costs for using the facility indicate that it would not be more a few thousand rupees per hour of broadcast. One major advantage of satellite broadcast is the quality of education that can be imparted as compared to that served up by impoverished, "third-rate" teachers in broken down primary schools. For NGOs the technology is appropriate for accurate targeting in any field of activity with relatively less problems of coordination and administrative support, resulting in speeding up the delivery process. One would like to propose, though, that we are now at that crucial juncture in our political and social development when the time has come to concentrate on empowering the hitherto marginalised sections of society by freeing them from the bondage of ignorance and enabling them to be the masters of their own lives.

Those of us who already stand in the sun, must make some place for those who still cower in the dark.

NOTES

Datta, Abhijit : Decentralisation and Local Government Reform in India. *The Indian Journal of Public Administration—Administrative Reforms Revisited*, July-September 1985, p. 562.

See Ramaswamy, Dr. A. S. : *Empowerment of People : Panchayati Raj and NGO Movement.* Kurukshetra, August 1994, p. 32.

World Bank : *World Development Report 1991 — The Challenge of Development*, p. 35.

Ibid., p. 56.

Gillis, Perkins, *Roemer and Snodgrass* : *Economics of Development*, Second Edition 1987, W. W. Norton & Company, NY and London, p. 210.

Goulet, Dennis : "Development" ... Liberation?, *International Development Review*, Vol. XIII, No. 3 (September 1971), reproduced in Wilber, Charles K., The Political Economy of Development and Underdevelopment, Random House, New York, 1984, p. 461.

See, for example, the brief examination of the issue in Clarence Zuvekas, Jr. : *Economic Development—An Introduction*, St. Martin's Press, New York, 1979, pp. 25-26.

See Dayal, Ishwar : "Improvinig Behaviour in Administration" in *IJPA*, July-September 1985, pp. 583-584.

For technical details on SITE, and the overall programme till the mid-1980's, see Jai P. Singh and K. Narayanan : "Broadcasting Satellite Service in India", *IEEE Journal on Selected Areas in Communications*, Vol. SAC-3, No. 1, January 1985.

Ibid., p. 237.

K. Narayanan and P. Ramachandran : *Satellite Communication Programmes for Rural Education and Development* in *Space and Developing Countries*, a special report of the World Space Congress, 1992, p. 37.

12

TRAINING OF COMMUNICATORS AND MEDIA PERSONS FOR IMPLEMENTATION OF MEDIA POLICY

Abdur Rahim

Should India have a national media policy? Do we already have one, evolved by accident rather than by intention. Does it have mechanism to review its anomalies, raise its public visibility, and confront the social issues raised by the new communications technology.

The future of media, like their past, depends on the actions of government, in all its forms. To suggest the need for a national media policy, in a society that cherishes free expression, conjures up disturbing images of potential thought control. Our present media policy is made up of the many regulations that affect the operations of media, existing and potential. That web of unrelated and sometimes inconsistent rules arises out of the separate histories and circumstances through which the individual media have evolved. It is constantly being adjusted and revised, by legislation, administrative actions and judicial rulings. Both the rules and the chances for inconsistency among them have multiplied as communication technology has grown more complex, the once well-defined boundary lines between different media have crumbled, and individual and mass communication increasingly share common delivery methods.

My purpose in this paper is to encourage long-range reflection on the implications of present policies, and to suggest the need for training of communication specialists and professionals for attaining the objectives and goals of our media policy. Given the rapid rate of change both in the media business and in the rules, it would be foolish to offer a comprehensive policy blueprint on subjects that are complex, enveloped in specialized technicalities, and, in some instances, intensely controversial.

Media are affected by government actions in spheres that at first glance seem to have nothing to do with communications at all; at the same time, the regulation of media often has repercussions in other areas of society. As communication technology grows and changes, the boundary lines that separated media in the past become increasingly difficult to sustain, and the need for new policies becomes more apparent. Paradoxically, a communications system that is easier and simpler for users to operate requires a more complex and costly technology. This problem has recently been brought into sharp focus by the huge investment required to replace existing digital system and the copper telephone lines with the latest state-of-the art fiber-optic network capable of handling, on a broad frequency band, a vast array of information and entertainment services. Since these would encompass both mass and private communication, a new set of policy issues has been raised regarding the relationship between public utilities being highly regulated at the local level and mass media protected by constitutional guarantees.

Before the end of the 20th Century, the impending spread of fiber-optic networks with broadband communications capabilities is destined to lower the artificial barrier between data processing and communication. It will also make obsolete the distinction that regulators had drawn among the various types of communications organisations, in or out of the mass media field.

Media content is not immune from government policy regulation. It is readily understandable why government should become involved in one way or another with the technical and business aspects of electronic media. The content of programming is an altogether different matter and represents a potential quagmire. Yet this is an area that government cannot and does not avoid altogether.

The involvement of government with media content is periodically expressed in an explosion of concern over media violence and pornography, and occasionally on the effect of advertising on children. If improving media quality is a desirable social objective, does this automatically suggest a role for the state in establishing and maintaining cultural standards? No requirements of ideological balance or objectivity have ever been set for the Indian press, nor has it ever been suggested that their content should be monitored to ensure that the public interest is nor being abused.

Should media that makes use of public goods be held accountable to some meaningful standard of public service, or should they be given free rein in the commercial market for entertainment and information?

Do we need a comprehensive national media policy? The mere prospect of attempting this is unsettling. The legal system continually weighs the often inherently contradictory contentions of justice and equity, and reinterprets received doctrine to meet the needs of changing times. It better serves the causes of free expression and of technological innovation to have the rules governing mass communication arise out of different components of government, dealing with individual cases, as in the common law, and with a variety of precedents to choose among, rather than to have them all assembled and written down in one place, like a Napoleonic Code. Still, the lack of clarity and consistency in the rules should not be supinely accepted.

National Media Commission

As we move toward the extraordinary communication challenges of the 21st century, it seems appropriate to consider the possibilities of instituting a process that might mesh, coordinate and smooth out the contradictions in our present anarchic national media policy. The device might be a National Media Commission. Its purpose would be to examine and review periodically inconsistencies and problems in the working of the present policies and to recommend remedial legislation.

A useful point of departure may be to attempt to articulate national goals for mass communication. These are :

(1) to encourage a variety of channels for expression;
(2) to discourage concentration of control over the channels of expression;
(3) to facilitate an extensive and fair exchange of ideas, and to protect society, and specially children—its most vulnerable members—from abuse; and
(4) to subsidize forms of exprêssion that enrich the mosaic of our national culture and its collective and diversified intellectual resources.

It is not likely that there is universal agreement on all these points. Vigorous discussion—and not just by experts—is precisely what media policy needs as it deals with ever more complex matters which have greater social repercussions.

I intend to raise two or three issues regarding Indian mass media so that we can understand the need for greater professionalism in media content and performance.

The Second Press Commission, (1982) said :

> It is to the credit of the Indian press that despite its predominantly urban and middle class moorings... from time to time, have drawn attention to such matters concerning the weakest sections of society as non-enforcement of minimum wages and to the failure to revise them, to keep pace with the fall in the purchasing power of the rupee, the persistence of bounded labour despite its abolition by law or its emergence in a new guise as contract labour; the generation of black money and its use, frequently entailing the involvement of corrupt officials and politicians... etc.

Can this conscience-raising role, which is crucial to human development, be claimed for the official communication media? Unlike the press, these are public-owned media subsidised from government revenue. Is it wrong to expect a more direct and more significant contribution from the official mass media? What could be the reason?

Is it their pre-occupation with the hardware of centralised and wide-spread transmission, to the neglect of problems of access to the media, its availability, local relevance of software and the linguistic and cultural distance of communicators from their audience? How can this distance be bridged if not through imparting basic skills and training in different dialects of languages. What happened to the proposals regarding a decentralised broadcasting system. The Report of the Working Group on Autonomy for Akashvani and Doordarshan (1978) said :

> Decentralized and participative development from below suggests the need for decentralized messages through local radio and TV... We envisage at the local leval a small and relatively simply equipped "mother station, with a cluster around it of small recording units and programming facilities, which will help bring broadcasting to the people and people to broadcasting. This consideration applies to both radio and television."

But the Indian audience, particularly the elite have tasted blood and they cannot be expected to give up TV entertainment as the latest addition to "the good things of life". And what has happened, we have over 580 HPTs and LPTs dotting our landscape today, beaming programmes for atleast 18 hours a day, supplemented by the foreign satellite transmissions and Cable TV, who give you round-the-clock service. Is there a lacunae somewhere in the way Indian TV has grown? Are there any policy implications that we need to seriously ponder over?

Another shadow area which still needs a lot of thinking out and what's more requires a lot of training, is the news policy for the broadcast media. The G. Parthasarathi Committee (1982) recommended certain guidelines, which was endorsed by the Government and issued to the AIR and Doordarshan. It stressed the importance of "the highest possible professional standards" in the selection and editing of news. It said "that while ministerial statements on policy matters, particularly those of the Prime Minister, are important, the focus should be on information rather than on individuals" and that "views critical of official policies and the manner of their implementation should find adequate time". Are AIR and Doordarshan following these sound principles in practice? The fault does not lie with the people handling the news, for they are upright bureaucrats. The fault lies with our professionals who lack the skills and training in making "an objective and fair presentation of the news about events, problems and issues, by covering them from the public point of view without any hesitation in bringing out healthy criticism".

Lastly, I cannot but comment on a specific aspect of our media policy regarding telecasting soaps and films and film-based programmes. Unlike a pornographic book or a journal read by an individual, or a sex-and-violence film viewed in the anonymity of a crowd in a dark and foul-smelling cinema hall, a film screened on TV is often watched by three generations of a family. And what do we see is the most repulsive exhibition of so private and personal experience like man-woman relationships. My objection is both to the vulgarity, "pelvic syndrome", but also to the all-out permisiveness portrayed, which is against the grain of Indian culture, its society and its mores, the "Neena Gupta syndrome". Yes, the burgeoning middle class might be more prudish and to many of us very hypocritical, but they form the bulk of the TV audience. This permissiveness which might exist in the lowest sections of society or the very rich, cannot be thrust upon the embarrased middle class audiences. Alas, we have yet not been able to provide selected programmes to a select audience over our National networks, though attempts are being made to restrict such programmes to late night, which is a cruel joke on the TV viewing audience. The basic reason why we have not been able to produce good, healthy and entertaining programmes, is like the tinsel world, the TV hacks have also adopted the "*masala*" approach. Trained professionals are the only answer to this growing trend of "*masala*" TV.

13

RESEARCH INPUTS IN COMMUNICATION POLICY

Vijayluxmi Bose

The communication policy is being framed at a time when media and communication technology has reached its peak. Satellite technology in particular has widened the reach of television; however, radio continues to have its following among those who listen to music, news and current affairs broadcasts. Those who cannot afford television still rely on radio for entertainment and information. In the field of computers, INTERNET has developed as 'wired broadcasting' (Karnik, 1995) through which anyone with access can be in touch with over 20 million households worldwide. Such a scenario is far from futuristic. The media policy comes at a time when India is already in the midst of a communication revolution and a policy framework is really necessary to provide a direction.

However, what should the policy be based on? The answer is—the present communication scenario and needs of the people. However, this is where the questions begin. What do we mean when we say 'the people'? Do we mean those who are consumers of media or do we mean those who are critical of the media? Have we any data on the way media influences 'peoples' lives, mores and ways of thinking and behaviour? More importantly in a multi-channel media situation, where cross-media ownerships are becoming the order of the day and commercial sponsorships are dictating programmes—does anyone know or care? What is commonly heard is the excuse that 'other channels have such programming' or 'people like viewing such programmes' without a research base to support or disprove such arguments.

From the research aspect what is needed, therefore, is much more data both quantitative and impressionistic about audiences : not only hard data about viewing habits but a deeper insight into their feelings and views about radio and television programmes. This research base needs to be constantly updated longitudinally in terms of time and situationally in terms of specific audience segments.

The communication policy cannot ignore the debates about the communication revolution which makes a case against the mesmerizing influence of television, against technologies which are further marginalizing the already deprived and creating demands that many cannot afford. Media policy makers when faced with the problem of what to do in face of these two lobbies needs to walk the tightrope.

The media policy must have inputs from the entertainment, 'infotainment' and 'entereducate' lobbies. In order to define what these mean to general audience there is a need to ask them the moot question—are they truly satisfied and what more do they want to view and listen to. In terms of research, this is fraught with the dangers of what researchers call 'social desirability'; since research conducted to date shows that people view what entertains them best and any opinion that is 'holy holy' and differs from the norm may be subjected to more in depth research because it may just be the recipe for the 'mix' that the media policy is looking out for.

There are two choices before the media planners—to let the current scenario (such as it is) inform the policy and then face the lobbies and counter lobbies, draft and redraft, or to take a step away from the actual drafting to see what the issues are and build a solid research base for the draft.

This then runs into the problem of time. Research is both time-consuming and expensive; while the findings are being analysed, the policy might become redundant! This then is the excuse which throws out the baby with the bath water and provides an easy escape route. The truth is that with time, communication research methods have also changed. There are ways in which one can obtain reliable data in a very short time. There are ways also where fresh research does not have to be commissioned but data can be gathered and fed into the policy. It is these methods which have to be explored as research inputs to the media policy.

The next set of questions pertains to the modes and methods of research. Over the years, communication research has evolved various methods both purely experimental and field-based. Significant among the national level experimental studies are the Countryside Classroom Talkback experiments done under the aegis of the ISRO-IGNOU collaboration. These did have an experimental group (which actually participated in the two-way video and one-way audio experiment) and control group (which saw the video but did not ask questions) design and indicated that given the time and cost involved, there was a certain amount of learning which took place. Such an experiment has relevance for the communication policy insofar as it indicates the way state-of-the-art communication technologies are viewed by audiences.

There are many examples of field based research involving specific television programmes, *Chowraha*, *Rajni* and the educative tele-serial on the girl-child *Meena* and good examples of the same. A recent study of the Media Advocacy group on the views of a cross-section of women when they viewed songs telecast in various film-based programmes is another relevant example.

Another truism that is often heard is—in order to get views of the general audience, research must be participatory. This can be operationalized only if media policy-makers consult NGOs and community based groups who actually are in touch with the people, have a certain amount of credibility and can yield micro-level data. However, data thus generated may not be easily generalisable. The question then is, in a country such as ours how far can one 'generalise'? Is it not time that we as researchers took a long hard look at what we have learnt in classrooms in light of what is needed at the field level? Unless this transition is completed, the media policy will reflect the views of those who are shut away in the ivory towers of esoteric research and not the views of the audience who (as I have seen in the slums of many cities) get together and pool their meagre earnings to gather around a television set.

Establishing a Task Force

How does one solve this dilemma—that on the one hand data is necessary and on the other, reliable data means time that the policy cannot afford? All across India, in departments of communication and extension, research is being conducted every year by postgraduate, M. Phil and Ph. D. students; data is being gathered on various media issues and problems. In addition to this, various ministries and international agencies commission research which may have an audience research component. The best idea would be to set up some kind of Task Force who would examine research and see whether parts or all of it could be fed into the Policy document. Incidentally, they would also be doing yeoman service to the discipline of communication research, in helping research to circulate within the discipline.

Time and money permitting, 'meta research' techniques could be used to tie up these studies into a macro study on which to base a part of the media policy. Another method that has already being done is the organisation of seminars and presentations after a study is completed.

This still leaves a major question unanswered—where are the 'people' whose feelings and opinions need to be put in the form of data? Indian has a large NGO/CBO Voluntary organisation structure which needs to be tapped in this regard. Recent years have seen many media NGOs who specialize in materials development and communication support. As a prelude to these activities, they do some kinds of community based communication needs analysis. Those micro-level researchers are necessary inputs into the media policy. Also, there are various lobbies which, if not heard now will make their voices heard when the policy is drafted. There is a need to approach them and find out exactly what it is that they would like to see in the Media Policy. Media researchers anyway are a strange mix of those who practice, those who preach, those who analyse and those who do a little of all three. The entire media community needs representation in the media policy if the policy is to be true to its canons.

Reconstitution of Programme Committees

A step in the right direction would be the reconstitution of the Programme Committees of A.I.R. and Doordarshan. The composition of the Committees should be changed to accommodate not only media persons, but NGO representatives, media consumers and others. This is a step in the right direction to get 'instant feedback' on the type of programmes which should be broadcast and telecast.

The choices before both the media planners, media people, academics and others is clear—either they can continue to discuss the 'foreign media' (all the while cable channels increase) or they can have a media policy that addresses all these issues and continues to do so; incorporates views, research, feelings, doubts and fears. Media policy in the changing media scenario cannot be static—and in order to reflect vox populi has to use research to go to the people.

14

PROCEEDINGS OF THE REGIONAL SEMINARS AND THE NATIONAL COLLOQUIUM

V. S. Gupta

REGIONAL SEMINARS

Chandigarh, 5-6 May 1995

The first seminar on National Media Policy was organised at Chandigarh on 5-6 May 1995.

Inaugurating the seminar, Mr. Dhanendra Kumar, Principal Secretary to the Chief Minister, Haryana, said that the media whether print, visual or audio, was on the threshold of a new era and its responsibility was not only to inform but also to prepare people for new challenges. Media, he said, should disseminate information and stimulate knowledge about various aspects of development like new technologies, preservation of environmental and ecological balances and measures of population control so as to achieve a certain degree of national initiative for maintaining communal harmony. He said, the Indian media policies had been influenced by two guiding principles. Article 19 of the Indian Constitution which guaranteed the right of freedom of speech and expression and the Universal Declaration of Human Rights according to which every one had the right to freedom of speech and expression.

The Deputy Editor, *The Tribune*, Mr. T. K. Ramaswamy, said that there could not be one media policy for all newspapers because of sharp differences in their circulation, reach, language, culture, milieu and local traditions. Actually, attempt to evolve a common policy would lead to the government tilting in favour of the big "national" dailies and leaning on the others. At present, what went for policy were essentially some old clauses in the Cr. P. C., Obscenity Act, Official Secrets Act, etc.

Ms. Nandini Prasad, Media Analyst, suggested that newspapers should reduce political coverage and give more space to professional writings on developmental and social issues. She stressed the need for a firm media policy particularly in respect of women's issues.

Participating in the seminar on the second day, Mr. Prem Kumar, veteran journalist, said besides updating technology there was need for paying more attention to the education and training of the media personnel. Whatever was being done was inadequate and at times irrelevant. People would soon demand of the media greater credibility, accuracy, objectivity, details, keener observation, more interesting description and scientific analysis.

Mr. Prem Kumar said development journalism had yet to come in the real sense. More qualified and trained persons would have to be engaged for this kind of coverage.

In her paper, "Communication Policies—An Overview", Ms. Vir Bala Aggarwal of the Department of Journalism and Mass Communication, Himachal Pradesh University, said that media policies should be sensitised to the issues relating to health, family planning and a disease free society. In fact, the policies should be so designed that they limit the percentage of foreign produced programmes.

On the concluding day of the seminar, diverse views were expressed on the need for a national media policy. While some of the participants maintained that the media should be better left alone and the government should not evolve a policy to regulate it, the others were of the view that without a policy, there can be no proper planning for media development in the country.

Prof. V. S. Gupta, AMIC Zonal Representative, in his concluding remarks, said the media policy should encourage the transfer of communication technology from the haves to the have-nots and the diversity of opinion should be accommodated under all circumstances.

The seminar was attended by 35 participants including journalists, media persons working in the government sector and faculty members from the related universities.

Bhopal, 9-10 September 1995

The Second Seminar was organized in collaboration with the Makhanlal Chaturvedi National University of Journalism at Bhopal on 9-10 September

1995.

In his inaugural speech, Deputy Chief Minister of Madhya Pradesh, Mr. Pyarelal Kanwar urged the media men to reach the rural masses of the country. He observed that the communication revolution would remain incomplete till such time as its benefits percolated to the rural population. He asked the media persons and experts to reach out of the remote tribal regions which will help proper study of socio-economic milieu of tribal areas, so important for the progress and development of the country. On this occasion, Mr. Kanwar released a book, *Rural Press — Problems and Prospects* edited by Prof. V. S. Gupta and Mr. Rajeshwar Dyal. The publication is based on papers presented at the three seminars on Rural Press Development held in different parts of the country during 1994.

The Director-General of the Institute, Mr. Arvind Chaturvedi underlined the need for awareness in people for greater participation in development programmes and pointed out that at present 5% persons decided the future of 95% of the population. The Media Adviser, FES, Mr. Rajeshwar Dyal underlined the need for rectifying the urban bias of the media. He observed that the media has become urban-biased instead of urban-based.

The seminar recommended the establishment of a Media Commission to formulate a National Media Policy for the country. On the second day, the Questionnaire on Media Policy circulated by the Ministry of Information and Broadcasting was discussed in detail. It was felt that the media policy should bridge the gap between the educated urban and the rural persons. Several participants pointed out that approach to the preparation of the questionnaire was wrong and it should have been finalized after consultation with media experts. It was also felt that the media policy should be implemented by a statutory body like Press Council of India or an Ombudsman consisting of the representatives of media organisations.

The concluding function was presided over by Mr. Rajender Prasad Shukla, Minister for Water Resources, Madhya Pradesh, who said that the media policy should strengthen the national values and ideals contained in our constitution.

The consensus in the seminar was that the media policy should be evolved by professional bodies. The seminar was attended by more than 30 participants including senior practising journalists, faculty members from journalim departments of over half a dozen universities and representatives of the local press.

Bangalore, 26-27 September 1995

The third seminar on National Media Policy was organised at Bangalore on 26-27 September 1995, in collaboration with Madhyam.

Inaugurating the seminar, the former Deputy Chief Minister, Karnataka, Mr. S. M. Krishna, called for a national debate on the forthcoming comprehensive broadcasting legislation, likely to be placed before the Indian Parliament. Mr. Krishna said the national debate should take place before the Lok Sabha elections so that it could become a referendum on an issue of national importance and be a part of the political agenda of all parties.

He welcomed the advent of private channels and even foreign newspapers since this heralded a good trend of competition. He wanted the Prasar Bharati Bill to be complete in all respects, as well as being comprehensive. Although a Bill of this kind was necessary, there was no gainsaying the fact that self-regulation was the best policy and which should find space in the comprehensive system.

Presiding over the inaugural session, the former Chief Justice of India, Mr. E. S. Venkataramaiah called for a national cultural and information policy that would involve journalists and people in the creative field. He also sought media participation in bridging the North-South divide as well as making the East less isolated from the rest of the country. The media had tremendous potential as a tool for creating awareness on the cultural aspect. The media's usefulness in countering the bane of over urbanisation, impoverishment of the rural areas and in propagating the relevance of Gandhian principles should not be overlooked, he said.

Mr. Justice Venkataramaiah said the interference from government, the monitoring of the official media by the agencies of the government did not bode well for the future of the autonomous media.

Reviewing the present media scenario in the country, the Acting Editor, *Economic Times*, Dr. Narendra Pani said : If you look at the extent of competition at all levels of journalism, the world today is fundamentally different from what it was even 10 years ago. Ten years ago, when policies were worked out by newspapers together, journalists went out to cover a story and decided what would be the lead and come back and everybody wrote the same thing in their own papers. So the whole element, the whole way of looking at it was not competitive. Today even if the number of papers is the same, the level of competition is very much greater at all levels—at the level of press, at the level of journalists, at the level of management, at the level of marketing, at the level of advertising, at all levels. Now this state of affairs, of media catering to the government, of a media that was not competitive, of a media focusing on politics and sustaining itself on patronage could not continue for one simple reason that as Indian democracy was growing, more and more people at lower levels, what we call the large middle class and what I behive today extends to even some of the lower strata, poorer economic levels in the society are looking for information, not just what the leadership wanted to give them. They are looking for independent levels of information. Referring to the increased competition at every level Dr. Pani said : So, the competition was, therefore, at the marketing level, at the journalist level, advertising level and even in terms of the size of the product. The role of the market has been so phenomenal that it is perhaps best seen on T. V. rather than the print media because even a government organisation like Doordarshan has fallen in completely with the requirement of marketing, completely with the requirements of advertising and completely with the requirements of making more money as and when possible.

The well known consumer movement activist, Ms. Shakuntala Narasimhan, referred to the conflict of interest evinced in the state run television set up in the country because on the one hand, they want to generate profits through sponsorships, advertisements, and the kind of programmes like film based, at the top ratings according to their surveys; and on the other hand moulding people's perceptions, giving them ideas about their rights, social awareness, etc. She also pointed out that although one could go to the Advertising Standards Council of India, based in Bombay, against the tall claims and unethical and misleading advertisements, but not many people know that any one can write to them if they find an advertisement unacceptable or offensive.

In his presentation on "Satellite Communication and Decision Making at the Panchayat Raj Level", Mr. Abhijit Sengupta, Joint Secretary, Department of Space, said if the weak and poor sections of society, especially in rural India are to take their rightful place in the sun, not remaining marginalised but entering the main stream of national policy, then it is necessary that a major thrust is given, as a policy effort towards removing the basic disabling factors of illiteracy and lack of opportunity. The major advantage of satellite broadcast is the quality of education that can be imparted as compared to that served up by impoverished teachers in broken down primary schools.

The Dean, Asian College of Journalism, suggested a code of ethics to be formulated by the media men themselves. He also suggested that the institution of Ombudsman must be legalised and all newspapers must appoint an Ombudsman who could be a senior newsman or a retired judge to look into the complaints of ethical misconduct.

The Special Correspondent, *Indian Express*, Sharita Rai suggested that a media policy for a country like India can ill-afford to focus media concerns in isolation from the integral development of the nation as a whole. The arbitrary and directionless growth of software is not likely to serve the cause of women in their emerging new roles towards the start of the 21st Century.

Rourkela, 14-15 October 1995

The fourth seminar in the series was organised at Rourkela in collaboration with the Orissa Chapter of the Public Relations Society of India. The Revenue and Transport Minister, Orissa, Mr. K. C. Lenka inaugurated the seminar.

In his inaugural address, Mr. Lenka appealed to the media to publish news only after proper verifications so that the press did not create a sense of demoralization in the society on the basis of exaggerated news of deprivation. The press should use the freedom of expression with due sense of responsibility and promote the ethos of development and positive values amongst the people.

Dr. S. Nanda, Professor, Department of Political Science and Public Administration, Sambalpur, made a detailed presentation on the right of freedom of speech and expression, and the Universal Declaration of Human Rights.

Mr. Abhay Padhi, Station Director, Akashvani, Sambalpur suggested that voluntary codes of conduct be evolved by various media institutions whose implementation should be looked after by the members themselves. He also suggested that proper compilation should be made of the important judicial pronouncements on different aspects of the working of the media and its implementation by the concerned authorities.

NATIONAL COLLOQUIUM

IIMC, New Delhi, 10-11 November 1995

The National Colloquium in New Delhi, hosted by the Indian Institute of Mass Communication on 10-11 November 1995 provided a fitting finale to the series of four regional seminars.

Inaugurating the National Colloquium hosted by the Indian Institute of Mass Communication, the Union Minister for Information and Broadcasting, Mr. P. A. Sangma said : A concrete and well-defined media policy aimed at articulating and harmonising vision about the future of India has become necessary in view of the revolutionary changes in the communication scenario. The fast shifting new media scene in respect of innovation and changes in communication technologies has caused nationwide demand for a media policy.

The Minister pointed out that while formulating a media policy, it had to be kept in mind that the new, exhaustive media policy would have far-reaching consequences on the country's socio-economic and cultural life. He said the proposed media policy should ensure continuity and enrichment of diversities and pluralities. A meaningful media policy should also ensure access to relevant information, education and entertainment to all people, with priority to those living in areas away from the mainstream. Mr. Sangma said : While most countries in Asia and South Asia are generally conservative in allowing freely the use of satellite-linked cable T. V., India is more liberal. The need was to actually make good use of enormous opportunities that new communication technologies provided.

Earlier, welcoming the Minister, Mr. P. Murari, Chairman, IIMC said that in a democratic country of the size of India, it was impossible to formulate a Media Policy which did not meet the requirement of the pluralistic and diverse society that India is.

The Resident Representative, Friedrich Ebert Stiftung, Dr. Heinz Bongartz, in his opening remarks, while appreciating the efforts of AMIC-India and the IIMC in jointly organising the National Colloquium, said that it was being organised at a very appropriate time when the media and communication scenario in India was changing at a tremendous speed, making the task of policy makers and media professionals a daunting one. The Friedrich-Ebert-Stiftung attached great importance to the deliberations of this colloquium. He hoped that the discussions among communication experts will go a long way in the formulation of the media policy, which at present was a priority item on the agenda of the government.

Freedom of Information

Speaking on policy issues in the context of freedom of expression, Dr. Bongartz said : There can not be two opinions that in the formulation of a media policy commitment to freedom of information should be given top priority. In the present day world, information is power. The rationale of the right to information lies in the basic principle of a democratic system, namely that the government functions with the consent of the people. This consent has to be, both free and informed, which is possible only when information is freely made available to the citizens. They need to be provided information from various angles and sources. Only then they can make intelligent decisions and contribute to governmental decision making process. For making democracy real and participatory, people should have information about the working of the government. There may be certain areas where the information may be restricted, but it has to be ensured that legitimate protection of information is not made a pretext for any cover-up efforts.

In the context of latest developments in the field of satellite broadcasting and cable television, Dr. Bongartz observed : Cable television has opened before us a wider world. It brings information about activities in various fields — political, economic, cultural, educational, scientific, technological, ecological, business, commerce, art, music and sports from different parts of the world. In short, it brings to our drawing room more or less the whole active world. This magic communication system, thus, has enlarged our vision, widened our outlook, enhanced our knowledge and catered to our various interests. It has broken national barriers and transformed a global unity. We are coming in increasing contact with the people of various countries, their geographical surroundings, their religious and cultural life, their behaviour and pursuits.

Earlier in his Introductory Remarks, the Country Representative, AMIC, Prof. V. S. Gupta said : We are all aware that the media scenario in the country is developing and growing very fast, and the media technologies are penetrating at a rapid pace. The dramatic changes in the scenario have been graphically underlined in one of the recent papers by the FES media Chief, Mr. Gunter Lehrke, in the conference on, Impact of New Information Technology on Broadcasting, National Economies and Social Structure :

> We are already seeing worldwide : infotainment instead of news, headlines instead of articles, show instead of analytical and enlightening reporting, reality TV instead of news, entertaining instead of concern. But we are also getting war, dying, starvation-live.

It is, therefore, all the more important that we should evolve proper national media policy keeping in view the social and cultural dimensions of the information technologies and the impact it has on the society as a whole.

Alluding to the widening gap between the information-rich and the information-poor, Prof. Gupta said : It is indeed sad that in vast tracts of rural India people are not even aware of the emerging Information Society in the country. When I pointed out at Chandigarh Seminar in May this year that the rural sections of the society have missed the bus, I was told that they say : "The bus has not come this side at all". All this has to be taken into account while formulating the National Media Policy. At the Bhopal Seminar there was a strong feeling amongst the participants that rural areas in the country as a whole are being neglected by the media and this needs to be rectified.

In his Message, the AMIC Secretary-General, Mr. Vijay Menon said : AMIC feels privileged to have been able, over a period of almost a quarter century to promote debate on media policy and to aid in the development of the region's media. AMIC's pioneering efforts were made possible by the support provided by the Government of Singapore and the Friedrich Ebert Stiftung. Acknowledging the contribution of FES to AMIC-India programmes, Mr. Menon observed : The FES has been an exemplary donor agency, supportive but non-interferring. Nowhere has this been better demostrated than in India. During the last three years and more, encouragement and support from the FES has enabled AMIC-India to embark on a communication programme comprising seminars and workshops, publications and research, with a national focus. A book on media laws and regulations and seminars on media policy are but two examples of the products of FES support. AMIC-India's schedule is by far the most active of any national programme. We would like to thank the FES and its Representative in India, Dr. Heinz Bongartz, for the unwavering support that has enabled AMIC-India scale new heights of achievement."

Chairing the session on Print Media, the Director of Press Institute of India, Mr. Ajit Bhattacharjea said that the new technology has contributed to the devaluation of the institution of the Editor and the credibility of the print media.

While referring to the current trend of owner-editors, Mr. Bhattacharjea said : The allurement of quick money and influence has attracted financiers with no professional training or commitment. Owner editors have proliferated. Editorial staff have little professional training. Headlines are exaggerated and often provocative. Correspondents often double as advertising and sales agents. The news is exaggerated and distorted, even fictionalised, to raise circulations with little concern for the impact on society. Smaller papers indulge in local black mail; others are published only to justify securing official advertisements which has become a source of corruption rather than of help to genuine small papers.

Countering Corruption

Referring to the corruption of journalists and editors by government functionaries, he observed : Another source of journalistic corruption is the practice of distributing expensive gifts at press conferences given by companies keen to secure publicity of their products, shares etc. Correspondents of financial papers are specially favoured. Economic liberalisation has led to a sharp rise in this practice with multinational companies even offering foreign trips to journalists. Ethical codes condemn such practices but they will be curtailed only if exposed and condemned by the Press Council and other professional bodies. Industrial and commercial organisations should be asked to stop this practice.

The former Director, IIMC, Mr. M. V. Desai suggested that the following principles ought to guide media planners and govern media policies. Their principal aim should be to enable the citizen to realise his or her potential best. This will be easier when :

1. the access to media output is more even;
2. the preparation of media output is participatory and their production democratic;
3. there is greater pluralism of ownership and control;
4. the media are organised professionally, and
5. they reflect India's unity in diversity.

In his presentation on National Policy for T.V. and Satcom, Mr. Kiran Karnik from the Discovery Channel, India observed that the new technologies have demolished the monopoly of State-run channels and rendered ineffective the laws and regulations that were framed in a different era. Further, the availability of channels originated from outside the country has led to worries about an 'invasion from the sky'.

Mr. Karnik suggested that the elements of a policy for television and satellite communication, which should obviously be part of a more comprehensive media policy, will cover the purpose/objectives, the role of the State, the type of regulatory framework, the structure of the TV system and the incentives and disincentives or enforcement mechanisms. Other aspects too may have to be covered.

Concluding his presentation, Mr. Karnik observed : A pro-active stance by the government and anticipatory (rather than reactive) legislation will go a long way in creating a healthy and vibrant satellite TV Industry and in channelising it towards fulfilling national goals.

Market Forces and Media Management

Referring to the process of economic liberalisation and rapid technological changes in the country, the session on, Market Forces and Media, the Senior Vice-President, Media Services, MacCann Ericson, Mr. P. V. Narayanamoorthy observed : The pace of change is being accelerated by technological changes sweeping the world. Earlier, India was isolated from these changes and any impact was felt only marginally.

The worldwide launch of "Windows 95" has demonstrated how this situation has changed. Nobody could have imagined, even last year, that this would be available simultaneously in London and Patna.

Mr. Narayanamoorthy suggested joint efforts to tackle the problems through various industry bodies—the Advertising Agencies Association of India, the Media Research Users Council, the Indian Newspaper Society and the Indian Society of Advertisers.

Speaking in the Concluding Session, Prof. V. S. Gupta expressed sense of deep gratitude to the Director, IIMC, Dr. J. S. Yadava, for his keen personal interest in hosting the Colloquium. He hoped that there would be far more opportunities for AMIC-India to have collaboration with IIMC in its future programmes. On behalf of AMIC-India, Prof. Gupta placed on record his appreciation for the Friedrich Ebert Stiftung in sponsoring the regional seminars and the National Colloquium; and to the participants for their presentations in different sessions.

ANNEXURE I

EXCERPTS FROM SUPREME COURT JUDGEMENT ON FREEDOM OF AIRWAVES

Secretary, Ministry of I. & B. v. Cricket Association, Bengal A.I.R.

(A) Constitution of India, Art. 19(1)(a), (2)— Freedom of speech and expression—Includes right to acquire and disseminate information—Right to disseminate—Includes right to communicate through any media, print, electronic or audio visual —Restrictions permissible on such rights:

Freedom of Speech and Expression

The freedom of speech and expression includes right to acquire information and to disseminate it. Freedom of speech and expression is necessary, for self-expression which is an important means of free conscience and self-fulfilment. It enables people to contribute to debates of social and moral issues. It is the best way to find a truest model of anything, since it is only through it, that the widest possible range of ideas can circulate. It is the only vehicle of political discourse so essential to democracy. Equally important is the role it plays in facilitating artistic and scholarly endeavours of all sorts. The right to communicate, therefore, includes right to communicate through any media that is available whether print or electronic or audio-visual such as advertisement, movie, article, speech etc. that is why freedom of speech and expression includes

---

AIR 1995 Supreme Court 1236

P. B. Sawant, S. Mohan and B. P. Jeevan Reddy, JJ.*

Civil Appeals Nos. 1429-30 of, 1995 (arising out of S. L. P. (Civil) Nos. 18532-33 of 1993), with Writ Petn. (C) No. 836 of 1993, D - 9-2-1995.

Secretary, Ministry of Information and Broadcasting, Govt. of India and others, Appellants v. Cricket Association of Bengal and others, Respondents.

WITH

Cricket Association of Bengal and another, Petitioners v. Union of India and others, Respondents.

freedom of the press. The freedom of the press in terms includes right to circulate and also to determine the volume of such circulation. This freedom includes the freedom to communicate or circulate one's opinion without interference to as large a population in the country as well as abroad as is possible to reach. The fundamental right can be limited only by reasonable restrictions under a law made for the purposes mentioned in Art. 19(2) of the Constitution. The burden is on the authority to justify the restrictions. Public order is not the same thing as public safety and hence no restrictions can be placed on the right to freedom of speech and expression on the ground that public safety is endangered. Unlike in the American Constitution, limitations on fundamental rights are specifically spelt out under Art. 19(2) of our Constitution. Hence no restrictions can be placed on the right to freedom of speech and expression on grounds other than those specified under Art. 19(2).*

Airwaves — Need to have Central Agency

There is no doubt that since the airwaves/frequencies are a public property and are also limited, they have to be used in the best interest of the society and this can be done either by a central authority by establishing its own broadcasting network or regulating the grant of licences to other agencies, including the private agencies. What is further, the electronic media is the most powerful media both because of its audio-visual impact, and its widest reach covering the section of the society where the print media does not reach. The right to use the airwaves and the content of the programmes, therefore, needs regulation for balancing it and as well as to prevent monopoly of information and views relayed, which is a potential danger flowing from the concentration of the right to broadcast/telecast in the hands either of a central agency or of few private affluent broadcasters. *That is why the need to have a central agency representative of all sections of the society free from control both of the Government and the dominant influential sections of the society.* But to contend that on that account the restrictions to be imposed on the right under Art. 19(1)(a) should be in addition to those permissible under Art. 19(2) and dictated by the use of public resources in the best interests of the society at large, is to misconceive both the content of the freedom of speech and expression and the problems posed by the element of public property in , and the alleged scarcity of, the frequencies as well as by the wider reach of the media. If

---

*The judgements are printed in the order in which they are given in the certified copy. Ed.

*P. B. Sawant J. (for himself and on behalf of S. Mohan J).

the right to freedom of speech and expression includes the right to disseminate information to as wide a section of the population as is possible, the access which enables the right to be so exercised is also an integral part of the said right.'

Monopoly over Broadcasting not Permitted

True democracy cannot exist unless all citizens have a right to participate in the affairs of the polity of the country. The right to participate in the affairs of the country is meaningless unless the citizens are well informed on all sides of the issues, in respect of which they are called upon to express their views. One-sided information, disinformation, misinformation and non-information all equally create an uninformed citizenry which makes democracy a farce when medium of information is monopolised either by a partisan central authority or by private individuals or oligarchic organisations. This is particularly so in a country like ours where about 65 per cent of the population is illiterate and hardly 1½ per cent of the population has an access to the print media which is not subject to pre-censorship. When, therefore, the electronic media is controlled by one central agency or few private agencies of the rich, there is a need to have a central agency, representing all sections of the society. Hence to have a representative central agency to ensure the viewers right to be informed adequately and truthfully is a part of the right of the viewers under Art. 19(1)(a).**

From the standpoint of Art. 19(1)(a), what is paramount is the right of the listeners and viewers and not the right of the broadcaster—whether the broadcaster is the State, public corporation, a private individual or body. A monopoly over broadcasting, whether by government or by anybody else, is inconsistent with the free speech right of the citizens. State control really means Governmental control, which in turn means, control of the political party or parties in power for the time being. Such control is bound to colour the views, information and opinions conveyed by the media. The free speech right of the citizens is better served in keeping the broadcasting media under the control of public. Control by public means control by an independent public corporation or corporations, as the case may be, formed under a statute. The corporation(s) must be constituted and composed in such a manner as to ensure its independence from Government and its impartiality on public issues. When presenting

---

*The judgements are printed in the order in which they are given in the certified copy. Ed.
**Per P. B. Sawant J. (for himself and on behalf of S. Mohan J.).

or discussing a public issue, it must be ensured that all aspects of it are presented in a balanced manner, without appearing to espouse any one point of view. This will also enhance the credibility of the media to a very large extent; *a controlled media cannot command that level of credibility. No monopoly of this media can be conceived for the simple reason that Art. 19(2) does not permit State monopoly unlike cl. (6) of Art. 19 vis-a-vis the right guaranteed by Art. 19(a)(g).**

The Indian Telegraph Act, 1885, was meant for a different purpose altogether. When it was enacted, there was neither Radio nor, of course, television, though it may be that radio or television fall within the definition of "telegraph" in S. 3(1). Except S. 4 and the definition of the expression "telegraph", no other provision of the Act appears to be relevant to broadcasting media. The Telegraph Act of 1885 is wholly inadequate and unsuited to an important medium like radio and television, i.e., broadcasting media. It is absolutely essential, in the interest of public, in the interests of the freedom of speech and expression guaranteed by Art. 19(1)(a) and with a view to avoid confusion, uncertainty and consequent litigation that Parliament steps in soon to fill the void by enacting a law or laws, as the case may be, governing the broadcasting media, i.e. both radio and television media.*

Curtailment of Freedom of Press by Unconstitutional Measures Liable to be Struck down

In Indian Express Newspapers (Bombay) Pvt. Ltd. v. Union of India (1985) 1 SCC641 : (AIR 1986 SC 515), the Court held that the expression "freedom of the press" has not been used in Article 19, but it is comprehended within Article 19(1)(a). This expression means a freedom from interference from authority which would have the effect of interference with the content and circulation of newspapers. There cannot be any interference with that freedom in the name of public interest. The purpose of the press is to advance the public interest by publishing facts and opinions without which democratic electorate cannot make responsible judgements. Freedom of the press is the heart of social and political intercourse. It is the primary duty of the Courts to uphold the freedom of the press and invalidate all laws or administrative actions which interfere with it contrary to the constitutional mandate. The freedom of expression has four broad social purposes to serve : (i) it helps an individual to attain self-fulfilment, (ii) it assists in the discovery of truth, (iii) it strengthens

*Per B. P. Jeevan Reddy, J.

the capacity of an individual in participating in decision-making and (iv) it provides a mechanism by which it would be possible to establish a reasonable balance between stability and social change. All members of the society should be able to form their own beliefs and communicate them freely to others. In sum, the fundamental principle involved here is the people's right to know. Freedom of speech and expression should, therefore, receive a generous support from all those who believe in the participation of people in the administration. It is on account of this special interest which society has in the freedom of speech and expression that the approach of the Government should be more cautious while levying taxes on matters concerning newspaper industry than while levying taxes on other matters. The Courts are there always to strike down curtailment of freedom of press by unconstitutional means. The delicate task of determining when it crosses from the area of profession, occupation, trade, business or industry into the area of freedom of expression and interferes with that freedom is entrusted to the Courts. In deciding the reasonableness of restrictions imposed on any fundamental right the Court should take into consideration the nature of the right alleged to have been infringed. The underlying purpose of the restrictions imposed, the disproportion of the imposition and the prevailing conditions including the social values whose needs are sought to be satisfied by means of the restrictions. *The imposition of a tax like the custom duty on news print is an imposition of tax on knowledge and would virtually amount to a burden imposed on a man for being literate and for being conscious of his duty as a citizen to inform himself of the world around him.* The pattern of the law imposing custom duty and the manner in which it is operated, to a certain extent, exposes the citizens who are liable to pay the custom duties to the vagaries of executive discretion.

David Feldman on Civil Libèrties

"Civil liberties and Human Rights" authored by David Feldman, the justification for and limits of freedom of expression are stated in the following words :

> The liberty to express one's self freely is important for a number of reasons. Firstly, self-expression is a significant instrument of freedom of conscience and self-fulfilment. Second justification concerns epistemology. *Freedom of expression enables people to contribute to debates about social and moral value. The best way to find the best or truest theory or model of anything is to*

> *permit the widest possible range of ideas to circulate. Thirdly, the freedom of expression allows political discourse which is necessary in any country which aspires to democracy. And lastly, it facilitates artistic scholarly endeavours of all sorts.*

The obvious connection between press freedom and freedom of speech is that the press is a medium for broadcasting information and opinion. Firstly, media freedom as a tool of self-expression is a significant instrument of personal autonomy. Secondly, as a channel of communication, it helps to allow the political discourse in a democracy. Thirdly, it helps to provide one of the essential conditions in scholarships making possible the exchange and evaluation of theories, explanations and discoveries, and lastly, it helps to promulgate a society's cultural values and facilities the debate about them, advancing the development and survival of civilisation.

Referring to the reasons for regulating the broadcasting media, the learned author has stated that first, the Government realises the potential of channels of mass communication for contributing to democracy or undermining it. *They hoped to foster a public service ethos in broadcasting so that it would be a medium for educating and improving the population. Secondly, in order to do this it was necessary to keep the media of mass communications from having programme policy dictated entirely by market forces.* A strong public sector and regulation of the independent sector when one started to operate were called for. Thirdly, when commercial broadcasters appeared on the scene, and a regulatory scheme was being developed for them, it was thought to be important to preserve a diversity of ideas by preventing oligopolistic concentrations of power in the hands of a few, usually rich and conservative media magnates, and to ensure that licences were granted only to people who could be expected not to abuse the privilege. The need to preserve propriety has been a motivating factor in the regulation of commercial broadcasting over much of the world. Fourthly, Government hoped to ensure that civilised standards were maintained, to uphold social values. Fifthly, wave lengths for broadcasting were limited. This purely technical consideration sharply distinguishes broadcasting from newspapers, and justifies a higher level of regulation. In theory, if not in practice, there is nothing to prevent any number of newspapers being published simultaneously. The only controlling mechanism needed is that of market forces. This is not true of broadcasting. Some control over the allocation of wavelengths is needed in order to ensure that they are sufficient for all legitimate broadcasters. Lastly, another legitimate object of national regulation is to protect the intellectual property rights of programme makers and broadcasters. It is permissible on his ground for an organisation to prevent people from getting access to programmes without paying proper licence fees. One way of preventing this is to encode programme transmissions and to restrict access to decoders to people who pay the fee.

Sporting Organisations are not Commercial Organisations

It must further be remembered that sporting organisations such as BCCI/CAB in the present case, have not been established only to organise the sports events or to broadcast or telecast them. The organisation of sporting event is only a part of their various objects, as pointed out earlier and even when they organise the events, they are primarily to educate the sportsmen, to promote and popularise the sports and also to inform and entertain the viewers. The organisation of such events involves huge costs. Whatever surplus is left after defraying all the expenses is ploughed back by them in the organisation itself. *It will be taking a deliberately distorted view of the right claimed by such organisations to telecast the sporting event to call it an assertion of a commercial right.* Yet the MIB has chosen to advance such contention which can only be described as most unfortunate. It is needless to state that we are, in the circumstances, unable to accept the ill-advised argument. *It does no credit to the Ministry or to the Government as a whole to denigrate the sporting organisations such as BCCI/CAB by placing them on par with business organisations sponsoring sporting events for profit and the access claimed by them to telecasting as assertion of commercial interest.*

There is no doubt that since the airwaves/frequencies are a public property and are also limited, they have to be used in the best interest of the society and this can be done either by a central authority by establishing its own broadcasting network or regulating the grant of licences to other agencies, including the private agencies. What is further, the electronic media is the most powerful media both because of its audio-visual impact, and its widest reach covering the section of the society where the print media does not reach. The right to use the airwaves and the content of the programmes, therefore, needs regulation for balancing it and as well as to prevent monopoly of information and views relayed, which is a potential danger flowing from the concentration of the right to broadcast/telecast in the hands either of a central agency or of few private affluent broadcasters. *That is why the need to have a central agency representative of all sections of the society free from control both of the Government and the dominant influential sections of the society. This is not disputed.* But to contend that on that account the restrictions to be imposed on the right under Article 19(1)(a) should be in addition to those permissible under Article 19(2) and dictated by the use of public resources in the best interests of the society at large is to misconceive both of the content of the freedom of speech and expression and the problems posed by the element of public property in, and the alleged scarcity of, the frequencies as well as by the wider reach of the media. *If the right to freedom of speech and expression includes the right to disseminate information to as wide a section of the population as is possible, the access which enables the right to be so exercised is also an integral part of the said right.*

ANNEXURE II

THE PRASAR BHARATI (BROADCASTING CORPORATION OF INDIA) ACT, 1990

No. 25 of 1990

[12 September, 1990]

An Act to provide for the establishment of a Broadcasting Corporation of India, to be known as Prasar Bharati, to define its composition, functions and powers and to provide for matters connected therewith or incidental thereto.

Be it enacted by Parliament in the Forty-first Year of the Republic of India as follows :

CHAPTER I

PRELIMINARY

Short Title, Extent and Commencement

1. (1) This Act may be called the Prasar Bharati (Broadcasting Corporation of India) Act, 1990.
   (2) It extends to the whole of India.
   (3) It shall come into force on such date as the Central Government may, by notification, appoint.

Definitions

2. In this Act, unless the context otherwise requires :

   (a) "Akashvani" means the offices, stations and other

establishments, by whatever name called, which, immediately before the appointed day, formed part of or were under the Director-General, All India Radio of the Union Ministry of Information and Broadcasting;

(b) "appointed day" means the date appointed under section 3;

(c) "broadcasting" means the dissemination of any form of communication like signs, signals, writing, pictures, images and sounds of all kinds by transmission of electro-magnetic waves through space or through cables intended to be received by the general public either directly or indirectly through the medium of relay stations and all its grammatical variations and cognate expressions shall be construed accordingly;

(d) "Board" means the Prasar Bharati Board;

(e) "Broadcasting Council" means the Council established under section 14;

(f) "Chairman" means the Chairman of the Corporation appointed under section 4;

(g) "Corporation" means the Prasar Bharati (Broadcasting Corporation of India) established under section 3;

(h) "Doordarshan" means the offices, kendras and other establishments, by whatever name called, which, immediately before the appointed day, formed part of or were under the Directorate-General, Doordarshan of the Union Ministry of Information and Broadcasting;

(i) "elected Member" means a Member elected under section 3;

(j) "Executive Member" means the Executive Member appointed under section 4;

(k) "kendra" means any telecasting centre with studios or transmitters or both and includes a relay station;

(l) "Member" means a Member of the Board;

(m) Member (Finance)" means the Member (Finance) appointed under section 4;

(n) "Member (Personnel)" means the Member (Personnel) appointed under section 4;

(o) "Nominated Member" means the Member nominated by the Union Ministry of Information and Broadcasting under section 3;

(p) "Non-lapsable Fund" means the Fund created from the commercial revenues of Akashvani and Doordarshan to meet expenditure on certain schemes;

(q) "notification" means a notification published in the Official

Gazette;

(r) "Part-time Member" means a Part-time Member of the Board appointed under section 4, but does not include an *ex officio* Member, the Nominated Member or an elected Member;

(s) "prescribed" means prescribed by rules made under this Act;

(t) "Recruitment Board" means a board established under sub-section (l) of section 10;

(u) "regulations" means regulations made by the Corporation under this Act;

(v) "station" means any broadcasting station with studios or transmitters or both and includes a relay station;

(w) "Whole-time Member" means the Executive Member, Member (Finance) or Member (Personnel);

(x) "year" means the financial year.

CHAPTER II

PRASAR BHARATI (BROADCASTING CORPORATION OF INDIA)

Establishment and Composition of Corporation

3. (1) With effect from such date as the Central Government may by notification appoint in this behalf, there shali be established for the purposes of this Act a Corporation, to be known as the Prasar Bharati (Broadcasting Corporation of India).

(2) The Corporation shall be a body corporate by the name aforesaid, having perpetual succession and a common seal with power to acquire, hold and dispose of property, both movable and immovable, and to contract, and shall by the said name sue and be sued.

(3) The headquarters of the Corporation shall be at New Delhi and the Corporation may establish offices, kendras or stations at other places in India and, with the previous approval of the Central Government, outside India.

(4) The general superintendence, direction and management of the affairs of the Corporation shall vest in the Prasar Bharati Board which may exercise all such powers and do all such acts and things as may be exercised or done by the Corporation under this Act.

(5) The Board shall consist of—

(a) a Chairman;
(b) one Executive Member;
(c) one Member (Finance);
(d) one Member (Personnel);
(e) six Part-time Members;
(f) Director-General (Akashvani), *ex officio*;
(g) Director-General (Doordarshan), *ex officio*;
(h) one representative of the Union Ministry of Information and Broadcasting, to be nominated by the Ministry; and
(i) two representatives of the employees of the Corporation, of whom one shall be elected by the engineering staff from amongst themselves and one shall be elected by the other employees from amongst themselves.

(6) The Corporation may appoint such committees as may be necessary for the efficient performance, exercise and discharge of its functions, powers and duties:
Provided that all or a majority of the members of each committee shall be Members and a member of any such committee who is not a Member shall have only the right to attend meetings of the committee and take part in the proceedings thereof, but shall not have the right to vote.

(7) The Corporation may associate with itself, in such manner and for such purposes as may be provided by regulations, any person whose assistance or advice it may need in complying with any of the provisions of this Act and a person so associated shall have the right to take part in the discussions of the Board relevant to the purposes for which he has been associated, but shall not have the right to vote.

(8) No act or proceeding of the Board or of any committee appointed by it under sub-section (6) shall be invalidated merely by reason of—

(a) any vacancy in, or any defect in the constitution of, the Board or such committee; or
(b) any defect in the appointment of a person acting as a Member or a member of such committee; or
(c) any irregularity in the procedure of the Board or such committee not affecting the merits of the case.

Appointment of Chairman and Other Members

4. (1) The Chairman and the other Members, except the *ex officio* Members, the Nominated Member and the elected Members shall be appointed by the President of India on the recommendation of a committee consisting of—

(a) the Chairman of the Council of States, who shall be the Chairman of the Committee;

(b) the Chairman of the Press Council of India established under section 4 of the Press Council Act, 1978; (37 of 1978); and

(c) one nominee of the President of India.

(2) No appointment of a Member shall be invalidated merely by reason of any vacancy in, or any defect in the constitution of, the committee appointed under sub-section (1).

(3) The Chairman and the Part-time Members shall be persons of eminence in public life; the Executive Member shall be a person having special knowledge or practical experience in respect of such matters as administration, management, broadcasting, education, literature, culture, arts, music, dramatics or journalism; the Member (Finance) shall be a person having special knowledge or practical experience in respect of financial matters and the Member (Personnel) shall be a person having special knowledge or practical experience in respect of personnel management and administration.

(4) The recommendations made by the committee constituted under sub-section (1) shall be binding for the purposes of appointment under this section.

Powers and Functions of Executive Member

5. The Executive Member shall be the Chief Executive of the Corporation and shall, subject to the control and supervision of the Board, exercise such powers and discharge such functions of the Board as it may delegate to him.

Term of Office, Conditions of Service, etc. of Chairman and Other Members

6. (1) The Chairman shall be Part-time Member and shall hold office

for a term of six years from the date on which he enters upon his office.

(2) The Executive Member, the Member (Finance) and the Member (Personnel) shall be Whole-time Members and every such Member shall hold office for a term of six years from the date on which he enters jupon his office or until he attains the age of sixty-two years, whichever is earlier.

(3) The term of office of Part-time Members shall be six years, but one-third of such Members shall retire on the expiration of every second year.

(4) The term of office of an elected Member shall be two years or till he ceases to be an employee of the Corporation, whichever is earlier.

(5) As soon as may be after the establishment of the Corporation, the President of India may, by order, make such provision as he thinks fit for curtailing the term of office of some of the Part-time Members then appointed in order that one-third of the Members holding office as such Part-time Members shall retire in every second year thereafter.

(6) Where before the expiry of the term of office of a person holding the office of Chairman, or any other Member, a vacancy arises, for any reason whatsoever, such vacancy shall be deemed to be a casual vacancy and the person appointed or elected to fill such vacancy shall hold office for the unexpired period of the term for which his predecessor in office would have held office if such vacancy had not arisen.

(7) The Whole-time Members shall be the employees of the Corporation and as such shall be entitled to such salaries and allowances and shall be subject to such conditions of service in respect of leave, pension (if any), provident fund and other matters as may be prescribed :

Provided that the salaries and allowances and the conditions of service shall not be varied to their disadvantage after their appointment.

(8) The Chairman and Part-time Members shall be entitled to such allowances as may be prescribed.

Removal and Suspension of Chairman and Members

7. (1) Subject to the provisions of sub-section (3), the Chairman or any other Member, except an *ex officio* Member, the Nominated

Member and an elected Member, shall only be removed from his office by order of the President of India on the ground of misbehaviour after the Supreme Court, on a reference being made to it by the President, has, on enquiry held in accordance with such procedure as the Supreme Court may by rules provide, reported that the Chairman or such other Member, as the case may be, ought, on such ground, be removed.

(2) The President may suspend from office the Chairman or other Member, except an *ex officio* Member, the Nominated Member or an elected Member, in respect of whom a reference has been made to the Supreme Court under sub-section (1) until the President has passed orders on receipt of the report of the Supreme Court on such reference.

(3) Notwithstanding anything contained in sub-section (1), the President may, by order, remove the Chairman or any Whole-time Member from his office if such Chairman or such Whole-time Member—

(a) ceases to be a citizen of India; or
(b) is adjudged an insolvent; or
(c) engages during his term of office in any paid employment outside the duties of his office; or
(d) is convicted of any offence involving moral turpitude; or
(e) is, in the opinion of the President, unfit to continue in office by reason of infirmity of body or mind :

Provided that the President may, by order, remove any Part-time Member from his office if he is adjudged an insolvent or is convicted of any offence involving moral turpitude or where he is, in the opinion of the President, unfit to continue in office by reason of infirmity of body or mind.

(4) If the Chairman or any Whole-time Member, except any *ex officio* Member, the Nominated Member or any elected Member, is, or becomes in any way concerned or interested in any contract or agreement made by or on behalf of the Corporation or the Government of India or the Government of a State or, participates in any way in the profit thereof, or in any benefit or emolument arising therefrom than as a member, and in common with other members of an incorporated company, he shall, for the purposes of sub-section (1), be deemed to be guilty of misbehaviour.

(5) If a Part-time Member is, or becomes in any way concerned, or interested in any contract or agreement made by or on behalf of the Corporation, he shall, for the purposes of sub-section (1), be deemed to be guilty of misbehaviour.

(6) The Chairman or any other Member may resign his office by giving notice thereof in writing to the President of India and on such resignation being accepted, the Chairman or other Member shall be deemed to have vacated his office.

Meetings of Board

8. (1) The Board shall meet at such times and places and shall observe such rules of procedure in regard to the transaction of business at its meetings (including the quorum at meetings) as may be provided by regulations :
Provided that there shall not be less than six meetings every year but three months shall not intervene between one meeting and the next meeting.

(2) A Member shall be deemed to have vacated his office if he absents himself for three consecutive meetings of the Board without the leave of the Chairman.

(3) The Chairman shall preside at the meetings of the Board and if for any reason he is unable to attend any meeting, the Executive Member and in the absence of both, any other Member elected by the Members present at such meeting, shall preside at the meeting.

(4) All questions which come up before any meeting of the Board shall be decided by a majority of the votes of the Members present and voting and, in the event of an equality of votes, the Chairman, or in his absence, the person presiding, shall have and exercise a second or casting vote.

Officers and Other Employees of Corporation

9. (1) Subject of such control, restrictions and conditions as may be prescribed, the Corporation may appoint, after consultation with the Recruitment Board, the Director-General (Akashvani), the Director-General (Doordarshan) and such other officers and other employees as may be necessary.

(2) The method of recruitment of such officers and employees and all other matters connected therewith and the conditions of

service of such officers and other employees shall be such as may be provided by regulations.

Establishment of Recruitment Boards

10. (1) The Corporation shall, as soon as may be, after the appointed day and in such manner and subject to such conditions and restrictions as may be prescribed, establish for the purposes of section 9, one or more Recruitment Boards consisting wholly of persons other than the Members, officers and other employees of the Corporation :

Provided that for the purposes of appointment to the posts carrying scales of pay which are not less than that of a Joint Secretary to the Central Government, the Recruitment Board shall consist of the Chairman, other Members, the *ex officio* Members, the Nominated Member and the elected Members.

(2) The qualifications and other conditions of service of the members constituting the Recruitment Board and the period for which such members shall hold office, shall be such as may be prescribed.

Transfer of Service of Existing Employees to Corporation

11. (1) Where the Central Government has ceased to perform any functions which under section 12 are the functions of the Corporation, it shall be lawful for the Central Government to transfer, by order and with effect from such date or dates as may be specified in the order, to the Corporation any of the officers or other employees serving in the Akashvani or Doordarshan and engaged in the performance of those functions :

Provided that no order under this sub-section shall be made in relation to any officer or other employee in the Akashvani or Doordarshan who has, in respect of the proposal of the Central Government to transfer such officer or other employee to the Corporation, intimated within such time as may be specified in this behalf by the Central Government, his intention of not becoming an employee of the Corporation.

(2) The provisions of sub-section (1) shall also apply to the members of the Indian Information Service, the Central Secretariat Service or any other service or to persons borne on

cadres outside Akashvani and Doordarshan who have been working in Akashvani or Doordarshan immediately before the appointed day :

Provided that where any such member intimates, within the time specified in sub-section (1), his intention of not becoming an employee of the Corporation but to continue on deputation, he may be allowed to continue on deputation in accordance with such terms and conditions as may be prescribed.

(3) In making an order under sub-section (1), the Central Government shall, as far as may be, take into consideration the functions which the Akashvani or, as the case may be, Doordarshan has ceased or ceases to perform and the area in which such functions have been or are performed.

(4) An officer or other employee transferred by an order under sub-section (1) shall, on and from the date of transfer, cease to be an employee of the Central Government and become an employee of the Corporation with such designation as the Corporation may determine and shall, subject to the provisions of sub-sections (5) and (6), be governed by such regulations as may be made as respects remuneration and other conditions of service including pension, leave and provident fund and shall continue to be an officer or other employee of the Corporation unless and until his employment is terminated by the Corporation.

(5) Every officer or other employee transferred by an order made under sub-section (1) shall, within six months from the date of transfer, exercise his option, in writing, to be governed—

(a) by the scale of pay applicable to the post held by him in the Akashvani or Doordarshan immediately before the date of transfer or by the scale applicable to the post under the Corporation to which he is transferred;

(b) by the leave, provident fund, retirement or other terminal benefits admissible to employees of the Central Government in accordance with the rules or orders of the Central Government, as amended from time to time, or the leave, provident fund or other terminal benefits admissible to the employees of the Corporation under the regulations.

and such option once exercised under this Act shall be final :

Provided that the option exercised under clause (a) by an officer or other employee shall be applicable only in respect of the post under the Corporation to which such officer or other employee is transferred and on appointment to a higher post under the Corporation he shall be eligible only for the scale of pay applicable to such higher post :

Provided further that if immediately before the date of his transfer any such officer or other employee is officiating in a higher post under the Government either in a leave vacancy or any other vacancy of a specified duration, his pay on transfer shall be protected for the unexpired period of such vacancy and thereafter he shall be entitled to the scale of pay applicable to the post under the Government to which he would have reverted or to the scale of pay applicable to the post under the Corporation to which he is transferred, whichever he may opt :

Provided also that when an officer or other employee serving in the Union Ministry of Information and Broadcasting or in any of its attached or subordinate offices is promoted to officiate in a higher post in the Ministry or office subsequent to the transfer to the Corporation of any other officer or employee senior to him in that Ministry or office before such transfer, the officer or other employee who is promoted to officiate in such higher post shall, on transfer to the Corporation, be entitled only to the scale of pay applicable to the post he would have held but for such promotion or the scale of pay applicable to the post under the Corporation to which he is transferred, whichever he may opt.

(6) No officer or other employee transferred by an order made under sub-section (1) or sub-section (2),—

(a) shall be dismissed or removed by an authority subordinate to that competent to make a similar or equivalent appointment under the Corporation as may be specified in the regulations;

(b) shall be dismissed or removed or reduced in rank except after an enquiry in which he has been informed of the charges against him and given a reasonable opportunity of being heard in respect of those charges :

Provided that where it is proposed after such enquiry to impose upon him any such penalty, such penalty may be imposed on the basis of evidence adduced during such enquiry and it shall not be necessary to give such person an opportunity of making representation on the proposed penalty :

Provided further that clause (b) shall not apply where an officer or other employee is dismissed or removed or reduced in rank on the ground of conduct which has led to his conviction on a criminal charge.

Functions and Powers of Corporation

12. (1) Subject to the provisions of this Act, it shall be the primary duty of the Corporation to organise and conduct public broadcasting services to inform, educate and entertain the public and to ensure a balanced development of broadcasting on radio and television.

Explanation—For the removal of doubts, it is hereby declared that the provisions of this section shall be in addition to, and not in derogation of, the provisions of the Indian Telegraph Act, 1885 (13 of 1985).

(2) The Corporation shall, in the discharge of its functions, be guided by the following objectives, namely :

(a) upholding the unity and integrity of the country and the values enshrined in the Constitution;

(b) safeguarding the citizen's right to be informed freely, truthfully and objectively on all matters of public interest, national or international, and presenting a fair and balanced flow of information including contrasting views without advocating any opinion or ideology of its own;

(c) paying special attention to the fields of education and spread of literacy, agriculture, rural development, environment; health and family welfare and science and technology;

(d) providing adequate coverage to the diverse cultures and languages of the various regions of the country by broadcasting appropriate programmes;

(e) providing adequate coverage to sports and games so as to encourage healthy competition and the spirit of sportsmanship;

(f) providing appropriate programmes keeping in view the special needs of the youth;

(g) informing and stimulating the national consciousness in regard to the status and problems of women and paying special attention to the upliftment of women;

(h) promoting social justice and combating exploitation, inequality and such evils as untouchability and advancing the welfare of the weaker sections of the society;

(i) safeguarding the rights of the working classes and advancing their welfare;

(j) serving the rural and weaker sections of the people and those residing in border regions, backward or remote areas;

(k) providing suitable programmes keeping in view the special needs of the minorities and tribal communities;

(l) taking special steps to protect the interests of children, the blind, the aged, the handicapped and other vulnerable sections of the people;

(m) promoting national integration by broadcasting in a manner that facilitates communication in the languages in India; and facilitating the distribution of regional broadcasting services in every State in the languages of that State;

(n) providing comprehensive broadcast coverage through the choice of appropriate technology and the best utilisation of the broadcast frequencies available and ensuring high quality reception;

(o) promoting research and development activities in order to ensure that radio and television broadcast technology are constantly updated; and

(p) expanding broadcasting facilities by establishing additional channels of transmission at various levels.

(3) In particular, and without prejudice to the generality of the foregoing provisions, the Corporation may take such steps as it thinks fit—

(a) to ensure that broadcasting is conducted as a public service to provide and produce programmes;

(b) to establish a system for the gathering of news for radio and television;

(c) to negotiate for purchase of, or otherwise acquire, programmes and rights or privileges in respect of sports and other events, films, serials, occasions, meetings, functions or incidents of public interest, for broadcasting and to establish procedures for the allocation of such programmes, rights or privileges to the services;

(d) to establish and maintain a library or libraries of radio, television and other materials;

(e) to conduct or commission, from time to time, programmes, audience research, market or technical service, which may be released to such persons and in such manner and subject to such terms and conditions as the Corporation may think fit;

(f) to provide such other services as may be specified by regulations.

(4) Nothing in sub-sections (2) and (3) shall prevent the Corporation from managing on behalf of the Central Government and in accordance with such terms and conditions as may be specified by that Government the broadcasting of External Services and monitoring of broadcasts made by organisations outside India on the basis of arrangements made for reimbursement of expenses by the Central Government.

(5) For the purposes of ensuring that adequate time is made available for the promotion of the objectives set out in this section, the Central Government shall have the power to determine the maximum limit of broadcast time in respect of the advertisement.

(6) The Corporation shall be subject to no civil liability on the ground merely that it failed to comply with any of the provisions of this section.

(7) The Corporation shall have power to determine and levy fees and other service charges for or in respect of the advertisements and such programmes as may be specified by regulations :
Provided that the fees and other service charges levied and collected under this sub-section shall not exceed such limits as may be determined by the Central Government, from time to time.

Parliamentary Committee

13. (1) There shall be constituted a Committee consisting of twenty-two Members of Parliament, of whom fifteen from the House of the People to be elected by the Members thereof and seven from the Council of States to be elected by the Members thereof in accordance with the system of proportional representation by means of the single transferable vote, to oversee that the

Corporation discharges its functions in accordance with the provisions of this Act and, in particular, the objectives set out in section 12 and submit a report thereon to Parliament.

(2) The Committee shall function in accordance with such rules as may be made by the Speaker of the House of the People.

Establishment of Broadcasting Council, Term of Office and Removal, etc. of Members Thereof

14. (1) There shall be established, by notification, as soon as may be after the appointed day, a Council, to be known as the Broadcasting Council, to receive and consider complaints referred to in section 15 and to advise the Corporation in the discharge of its functions in accordance with the objectives set out in section 12.

(2) The Broadcasting Council shall consist of—

(i) a President and ten other members to be appointed by the President of India from amongst persons of eminence in public life;

(ii) four Members of Parliament, of whom two from the House of the People to be nominated by the Speaker thereof and two from the Council of States to be nominated by the Chairman thereof.

(3) The President of the Broadcasting Council shall be a whole-time member and every other member shall be a part-time member and the President or the part-time member shall hold office as such for a term of three years from the date on which he enters upon his office.

(4) The Broadcasting Council may constitute such number of Regional Councils as it may deem necessary to aid and assist the Council in the discharge of its functions.

(5) The President of the Broadcasting Council shall be entitled to such salary and allowances and shall be subject to such conditions of service in respect of leave, pension (if any), provident fund and other matters as may be prescribed :

Provided that the salary and allowances and the conditions of service shall not be varied to the disadvantage of the President of the Broadcasting Council after his appointment.

(6) The other members of the Broadcasting Council and the

members of the Regional Councils constituted under sub-section (4) shall be entitled to such allowances as may be prescribed.

Jurisdiction of, and the Procedure to be Followed by, Broadcasting Council

15. (1) The Broadcasting Council shall receive and consider complaints from—

(i) any person or group of persons alleging that a certain programme or broadcast or the functioning of the Corporation in specific cases or in general is not in accordance with the objectives for which the Corporation is established;

(ii) any person (other than an officer or employee of the Corporation) claiming himself to have been treated unjustly or unfairly in any manner (including unwarranted invasion of privacy, misrepresentation, distortion or lack of objectivity) in connection with any programme broadcast by the Corporation.

(2) A complaint under sub-section (1) shall be made in such manner and within such period as may be specified by regulations.

(3) The Broadcasting Council shall follow such procedure as it thinks fit for the disposal of complaints received by it.

(4) If the complaint is found to be justified either wholly or in part, the Broadcasting Council shall advise the Executive Member to take appropriate action.

(5) If the Executive Member is unable to accept the recommendation of the Broadcasting Council, he shall place such recommendation before the Board for its decision thereon.

(6) If the Board is also unable to accept the recommendation of the Broadcasting Council, it shall record its reasons therefore and inform the Broadcasting Council accordingly.

(7) Notwithstanding anything contained in sub-sections (5) and (6), where the Broadcasting Council deems it appropriate, it may, for reasons to be recorded in writing, require the Corporation to broadcast its recommendations with respect to a complaint in such manner as the Council may deem fit.

CHAPTER III

ASSETS, FINANCES AND ACCOUNTS

Transfer of Certain Assets, Liabilities, etc., of Central Government to Corporation

16. As from the appointed day,—

(a) all property and assets (including the Non-lapsable Fund) which immediately before that day vested in the Central Government for the purpose of Akashvani or Doordarshan or both shall stand transferred to the Corporation on such terms and conditions as may be determined by the Central Government and the book value of all such property and assets shall be treated as the capital provided by the Central Government to the Corporation;

(b) all debts, obligations and liabilities incurred, all contracts entered into and all matters and things engaged to be done by, with or for the Central Government immediately before such day for or in connection with the purposes of Akashvani or Doordarshan or both shall be deemed to have been incurred, entered into and engaged to be done by, with or for the Corporation;

(c) all sums of money due to the Central Government in relation to the Akashvani or Doordarshan or both immediately before such day shall be deemed to be due to the Corporation;

(d) all suits and other legal proceedings instituted or which could have been instituted by or against the Central Government immediately before such day for any matter in relation to the Akashvani or Doordarshan or both may be continued or instituted by or against the Corporation.

Grants, etc., by Central Government

17. For the purposes of enabling the Corporation to discharge its functions efficiently under this Act, the Central Government may, after due appropriation made by Parliament by law in this behalf, pay to the Corporation in each financial year,—

(i) the proceeds of the broadcast receiver licence fees, if any, as reduced by the collection charges; and

(ii) such other sums of money as that Government considers necessary.

by way of equity, grant-in-aid or loan.

Fund of Corporation

18. (1) The Corporation shall have its own Fund and all the receipts of the Corporation (including the amounts which stand transferred to the Corporation under section 16) shall be credited to the Fund and all payments by the Corporation shall be made therefrom.

(2) All moneys belonging to the Fund shall be deposited in one or more nationalised banks in such manner as the Corporation may decide.

(3) The Corporation may spend such sums as it thinks fit for performing its functions under this Act and such sums shall be treated as expenditure payable out of the Fund of the Corporation.

Explanation—For the purposes of this section, "nationalised bank" means a corresponding new bank specified in the First Schedule to the Banking Companies (Acquisition and Transfer of Undertakings) Act, 1970 (5 of 1970) or a corresponding new bank specified in the First Schedule to the Banking Companies (Acquisition and Transfer of Undertakings) Act, 1980 (40 of 1980).

Investment of Moneys

19. The Corporation may invest its moneys in the securities of the Central Government or any State Government or in such other manner as may be prescribed.

Annual Financial Statement of the Corporation

20. (1) The Corporation shall prepare, in each financial year, an Annual Financial Statement for the next financial year showing separately—

(a) the expenditure which is proposed to be met from the

internal resources of the Corporation; and

(b) the sums required from the Central Government to meet other expenses, and distinguishing—

(i) revenue expenditure from other expenditure; and

(ii) non-plan expenditure from plan expenditure.

(2) The Annual Financial Statement shall be prepared in such form and forwarded at such time to the Central Government for its approval as may be agreed to by that Government and the Corporation.

Accounts and Audit of Corporation

21. (1) The Corporation shall maintain proper accounts and other relevant records and prepare an annual statement of accounts in such form and in such manner as may be prescribed.

(2) The accounts of the Corporation shall be audited by the Comptroller and Auditor-General of India at such intervals as may be specified by him and any expenditure incurred in connection with such audit shall be payable by the Corporation to the Comptroller and Auditor-General.

(3) The Comptroller and Auditor-General and any person appointed by him in connection with the audit of the accounts of the Corporation shall have the same rights and privileges and authority in connection with such audit as the Comptroller and Auditor-General has in connection with the audit of Government accounts and, in particular, shall have the right to demand the production of books, accounts, connected vouchers and other documents and papers and to inspect any of the offices of the Corporation.

(4) The accounts of the Corporation as certified by the Comptroller and Auditor-General of India or any other person appointed by him in this behalf together with the audit report thereon shall be forwarded annually to the Central Government and that Government shall cause the same to be laid before each House of Parliament.

Corporation not Liable to be Taxed

22. Notwithstanding anything contained in the Income-tax Act, 1961

(43 of 1961), or any other enactment for the time being in force relating to income-tax or any other tax on income, profits or gains, the Corporation shall not be liable to pay any income-tax or any other tax in respect of—

(a) any income, profits or gains, accruing or arising out of the Fund of the Corporation or any amount received in that Fund; and
(b) any income, profits or gains, derived or any amount received, by the Corporation.

CHAPTER IV

Miscellaneous

Power of Central Government to Give Directions

23. (1) The Central Government may, from time to time as and when occasion arises, issue to the Corporation such directions as it may think necessary in the interests of the sovereignty, unity and integrity of India or the security of the State or preservation of public order requiring it not to make a broadcast on a matter specified in the direction or to make a broadcast on any matter of public importance specified in the direction.

(2) Where the Corporation makes a broadcast in pursuance of the direction issuesd under sub-section (1), the fact that such broadcast has been made in pursuance of such direction may also be announced along with such broadcast, if the Corporation so desires.

(3) A copy of every direction issued under sub-section (1) shall be laid before each House of Parliament.

Power of Central Government to Obtain Information

24. The Central Government may require the Corporation to furnish such information as that Government may consider necessary.

Report to Parliament in Certain Matters and Recommendations as to Action Against the Board

25. (1) Where the Board persistently makes default in complying with

any directions issued under section 23 or fails to supply the information required under section 24, the Central Government may prepare a report thereof and lay it before each House of Parliament for any recommendation thereof as to any action (including supersession of the Board) which may be taken against the Board.

(2) On the recommendation of the Parliament, the President may by notification supersede the Board for such period not exceeding six months as may be specified in the notification :

Provided that before issuing the notification under this sub-section, the President shall give a reasonable opportunity to the Board to show cause as to why it should not be superseded and shall consider the explanations and objections, if any, of the Board.

(3) Upon the publication of the notification under sub-section (2)—

(a) all the Members shall, as from the date of supersession, vacate their offices as such;

(b) all the powers, functions and duties which may, by or under the provisions of this Act be exercised or discharged by or on behalf of the Board, shall, until the Board is reconstituted under this Act, be exercised and discharged by such person or persons as the President may direct.

(4) On the expiration of the period of supersession specified in the notification issued under sub-section (2), the President may reconstitute the Board by fresh appointments, and in such a case any person who had vacated his office under clause (a) of sub-section (3) shall not be disqualified for appointment :

Provided that the President may, at any time before the expiration of the period of supersession, take action under this sub-section.

(5) The Central Government shall cause the notification issued under sub-section (2) and a full report of the action taken under this section to be laid before each House of Parliament.

Office of Member not to Disqualify a Member of Parliament

26. It is hereby declared that the office of the member of the Broadcasting Council or of the Committee constituted under section 13 shall not disqualify its holder for being chosen as, or for being, a Member of

either House of Parliament.

Chairman, Members, etc., to be Public Servants

27. The Chairman and every other Member, every officer or other employee of the Corporation and every member of a Committee thereof, the President and every member of the Broadcasting Council or every member of a Regional Council or a Recruitment Board shall be deemed to be a public servant within the meaning of section 21 of the Indian Penal Code, (45 of 1860).

Protection of Action Taken in Good Faith

28. No suit or other legal proceeding shall lie against the Corporation, the Chairman or any Member or officer or other employee thereof or the President or a member of the Broadcasting Council or a member of a Regional Council or a Recruitment Board for anything which is in good faith done or intended to be done in pursuance of this Act or of any rules or regulations made thereunder.

Authentication of Orders and Other Instruments of Corporation

29. All orders and decisions of the Corporation shall be authenticated by the signature of the Chairman or any other Member authorised by the Corporation in this behalf and all other instruments executed by the Corporation shall be authenticated by the signature of the Executive Member or by any officer of the Corporation authorised by him in this behalf.

Delegation of Powers

30. The Corporation may, by general or special order, delegate to the Chairman or any other Member or to any officer of the Corporation, subject to such conditions and limitations, if any, as may be specified therein, such of its powers and duties under this Act as it may deem fit.

Annual Report

31. (1) The Corporation shall prepare once in every calendar year, in such form and within such time as may be prescribed, an annual

report giving a full account of its activities (including the recommendations and suggestions made by the Broadcasting Council and the action taken thereon) during the previous year and copies thereof shall be forwarded to the Central Government and that Government shall cause the same to be laid before each House of Parliament.

(2) The Broadcasting Council shall prepare once in every calendar year, in such form and within such time as may be prescribed, an annual report giving a full account of its activities during the previous year and copies thereof shall be forwarded to the Central Government and that Government shall cause the same to be laid before each House of Parliament.

Power to Make Rules

32. (1) The Central Government may, by notification, make rules for carrying out the provisions of this Act.

(2) In particular, and without prejudice to the generality of the foregoing power, such rules may provide for all or any of the following matters, namely :

(a) The salaries and allowances and conditions of service in respect of leave, pension (if any), provident fund and other matters in relation to the Whole-time Members under sub-section (7) of section 6;

(b) the allowances payable to the Chairman and Part-time Members under sub-section (3) of section 6;

(c) the control, restriction and conditions subject to which the Corporation may appoint officers and other employees under sub-section (1) of section 9;

(d) the manner in which and the conditions and restrictions subject to which a Recruitment Board may be established under sub-section (1) of section 10;

(e) the qualifications and other conditions of service of the members of a Recruitment Board and their period of office under sub-section (2) and section 10;

(f) the terms and conditions in accordance with which the deputation may be regulated under sub-section (2) of section 11;

(g) the salary and allowances and conditions of service in respect of leave, pension (if any), provident fund and other matters in relation to the President of the Broadcasting Council under sub-section (5) of section 14;

(h) the allowances payable to other members of the Broadcasting Council and the members of the Regional Councils, under sub-section (6) of section 14;

(i) the manner in which the Corporation may invest its moneys under section 19;

(j) the form and the manner in which the annual statement of accounts shall be prepared under sub-section (1) of section 21;

(k) the form in which, and the time within which, the Corporation and the Broadcasting Council shall prepare their annual report under section 31;

(l) any other matter which is required to be, or may be, prescribed.

Power to Make Regulations

33. (1) The Corporation may, by notification, make regulations not inconsistent with this Act and the rules made thereunder for enabling it to perform its functions under this Act.

(2) Without prejudice to the generality of the foregoing power such regulations may provide for all or any of the following matters, namely :

(a) the manner in which and the purposes for which the Corporation may associate with itself any person under sub-section (7) of section 3;

(b) the times and places at which meetings of the Board shall be held and, the procedure to be followed thereat, and the quorum necessary for the transaction of the business at a meeting of the Board under sub-section (1) of section 8;

(c) the methods of recruitment and conditions of service of officers and other employees of the Corporation under sub-section (2) of section 9;

(d) the remuneration and other conditions of service, including pension, leave and provident fund in relation to an officer or other employee of the Corporation under sub-section (4) of section 11;

(e) the authority competent to make certain appointments referred to in clause (a) of sub-section (6) of section 11;

(f) the services which may be provided by the Corporation under clause (f) of sub-section (3) of section 12;

(g) the determination and levy of fees and other service charges in respect of advertisements and other programmes under sub-section (7) of section 12;

(h) the manner in which and the period within which complaints may be made under sub-section (2) of section 15;

(i) any other matter in respect of which provision is, in the opinion of the Corporation, necessary for the performance of its functions under this Act :

Provided that the regulations under clause (c) or clause (d) shall be made only with the prior approval of the Central Government.

Rules and Regulations to be Laid Before Parliament

34. Every rule and every regulation made under this Act shall be laid, as soon as may be after it is made, before each House of Parliament, while it is in session for a total period of thirty days which may be comprised in one session or in two or more successive sessions, and if, before the expiry of the session immediately following the session or the successive sessions aforesaid, both Houses agree in making any modification in the rule or regulation, or both Houses agree that the rule or regulation should not be made, the rule or regulation shall thereafter have effect only in such modified form or be of no effect, as the case may be; so, however, that any such modification or annulment shall be without prejudice to the validity of anything previously done under that rule or regulation.

Power to Remove Difficulties

35. If any difficulty arises in giving effect to the provisions of this Act, the Central Government may, by order, published in the Official Gazette, make such provisions, not inconsistent with the provisions of this Act, as it may deem necessary, for the removal of the difficulty :

Provided that no such order shall be made after the expiry of a period of three years from the appointed day.

ANNEXURE III

POLICY GUIDELINES FOR OFFICIAL MEDIA

1. The Government is committed towards the establishment of an egalitarian society and to promote social and economic justice for all in the country. The official media units have to play a vital role in the context of overall development strategies and programmes of the Government. The various processes of thinking, planning and execution of publicity programmes have to be tuned to the efforts in these directions. People have to be mobilised towards the goals set by the Government and public support mustered for the programmes. The official media have, therefore, an obligation to provide information and build up motivation in support of such programmes and policies. It is in this context that the activities for the media should become an input in the nation building tasks. They must strengthen the confidence of the people, promote the concept of self-reliance and encourage forces of unity and national harmony.
2. All this has to be done by the official media with a certain degree of creativity, originality and ingenuity so that the official media remain credible as well as interesting to all sections of the society and specially the youth of the country.
3. The Government have in this context carefully considered and approved the following guidelines for assisting the various official media units in their functioning :

   (i) Media units should give effective coverage to Government's programmes, policies and achievements. Particular attention

---

Reproduced below is the letter issued by the Ministry of Information and Broadcasting on 2 July 1980 to the heads of the media units. Initially classified as 'confidential', it was placed before the Lok Sabha on 12 August 1980 and before the Rajya Sabha on 16 March 1981.

should be given to programmes and dissemination of information relating to developmental activities in all their facets including, for example, extension work in Agriculture, Education, Health and Family Welfare and Science and Technology.

(ii) Media units should devise and present suitable programmes relating to youth, including information regarding opportunities for and generation of employment in various fields.

(iii) Vigorous steps should be taken by the official media units to serve the rural population, minority communities, women, children, illiterate as well as other weaker and vulnerable sections of the society.

(iv) Each media unit should try to encourage both individual as well as collective effort by the handicapped, such as blind, deaf, dumb and other disabled persons as well as institutions doing service to this section of society. Media units should also try to propagate the good work that is being done to eradicate diseases like leprosy and to remove inhibitions about them.

(v) The media units should devise suitable programmes to eradicate social evils such as untouchability, narrow parochial attitudes and loyalties, inequalities and exploitation. Steps taken by the Government in this regard should be highlighted.

(vi) Dissemination of information, news and comments in Akashvani and Doordarshan and Films Division should be done in a fair, objective and balanced manner including contrasting points of view, with emphasis on events and developments. Reference to personalities may be made primarily for providing human interest.

(vii) Media units should adopt a professional approach in their activities. They should strive for creating audience interest and to meet their needs and expectations by talking about what is on the ground; having stories of local interest in a realistic manner by adopting actual field-based coverage. The Media units should, instead of limiting themselves mostly to what the Government is planning to do, identify and highlight successful examples of group and individual efforts in developmental activities and towards solutions of local problems. Problems and issues should also be covered from the public point of view without any hesitation in bringing out healthy criticism.

(viii) Media units, and particularly Akashvani and Doordarshan, should endeavour to put out news and features which are investigative and in depth. There should be a greater attempt in diversification of coverage in terms of personalities being brought in for participation, places of origination of news, and sources being relied upon.

(ix) Media units should have a constant dialogue among themselves and establish effective horizontal linkages to support and supplement one another's programmes and resources.

(x) Each media unit should have adequate systems for continuous evaluation and re-assessment of its performance in the context of its specific objectives, resources and schedules.

ANNEXURE IV

BROADCAST CODE GOVERNING ALL INDIA RADIO

We recognize the immense power of Radio and Television for both good and evil and the solemn responsibilities this places upon all broadcasters.

We believe, there, that the following cardinal principles should be enshrined in the policy and practice of all Broadcasting and Television organizations :

— To ensure the objective presentation of news and fair and unbiased comment;

— To promote the advancement of education and culture;

— To raise and maintain high standards of decency and decorum in all programmes;

— To provide programmes for the young which, by variety and content, will inculcate the principles of good citizenship;

— To promote communal harmony, religious tolerance and international understanding;

— To treat controversial public issues in an impartial and dispassionate manner;

— To respect human rights and dignity.

This Code was adopted by the Fourth Asian Broadcasters' Conference convened at Kuala Lumpur in 1962 and to which All India Radio was a party.

ANNEXURE V

CODE OF ADVERTISING PRACTICE OF THE ADVERTISING STANDARDS COUNCIL OF INDIA

CHAPTER - I

To Ensure the Truthfulness and Honesty of Representations and Claims Made by Advertisements and to Safeguard against Misleading Advertisements.

1. Advertisements must be truthful. All descriptions, claims and comparisons which relate to matters of objectively ascertainable fact should be capable of substantiation. Advertisers and advertising agencies are required to produce such substantiation as and when called upon to do so by The Advertising Standards Council of India.
2. Where advertising claims are expressly stated to be based on or supported by independent research or assessment, the source and date of this should be indicated in the advertisement.
3. Advertisements should not contain any reference to any person, firm or institution without due permission; nor should a picture of any generally identifiable person be used in advertising without due permission.
4. Advertisements shall not distort facts nor mislead the consumer by means of implications or omissions. Advertisements shall not contain statements or visual presentations which directly or by implication or by omission or by ambiguity or by exaggeration are likely to mislead the consumer about the product advertised or the advertiser or about any other product or advertiser.
5. Advertisements shall not be so framed as to abuse the trust of consumers or exploit their lack of experience or knowledge. No advertisement shall be permitted to contain any claim so exaggerated as to lead to grave or widespread disappointment in

the minds of consumers. For example :

(a) Products shall not be described as 'free' where there is any direct cost to the consumer other than the actual cost of any delivery, freight or postage. Where such costs are payable by the consumer a clear statement that this is the case shall be made in the advertisement.

(b) Where a claim is made that if one product is purchased another product will be provided 'free', the advertiser is required to show as and when called upon by The Advertising Standards Council of India that the price paid by the consumer for the product which is offered for purchase with the advertised incentive is no more than the prevalent price of the product without the advertised incentive.

(c) Claims which use expressions such as 'Up to five years' guarantee' or 'Prices from as low as Y' are not acceptable if there is a likelihood of the consumer being misled either as to the extent of the availability or as to the applicability of the benefits offered.

(d) Special care and restraint has to be exercised in advertisements addressed to those suffering from weakness, any real or perceived inadequacy of any physical attributes such as height or bust development, obesity, illness, impotence. infertility, baldness and the like to ensure that claims or representations, directly or by implication, do not exceed what is considered prudent by generally accepted standards or medical practice and the actual efficacy of the product.

(e) Advertisements inviting the public to invest money shall not contain statements which may mislead the consumer in respect of the security offered, rates of return or terms of amortization; where any of the foregoing elements are contingent upon the continuance of or change in existing conditions, or any other assumptions, such conditions or assumptions must be clearly indicated in the advertisements.

(f) Advertisements inviting the public to take part in lotteries of prize competitions permitted under the law or which hold out the prospects of gifts shall state clearly all material conditions so as to enable the consumers to obtain a true and fair view of their prospects in such activity. Further, such advertiser shall make adequate provisions for the judging of such competitions, announcement of the results and the fair distribution of prizes or gifts according to the advertised terms and conditions within a reasonable period of time. With regard to the announcement of results, it is clarified that the advertiser's responsibility under this section of the Code is discharged adequately if the advertiser publicizes the main result in the media used to announce the competition as far as is practicable, and advises the individual winners by post.

6. Obvious untruths or exaggerations intended to amuse or to catch the eye of the consumer are permissible, provided that they are clearly to be seen as humorous or hyperbolic and not likely to be understood as making literal or misleading claims for the advertised product.

CHAPTER - II

To Ensure that Advertisements are not Offensive to Generally Accepted Standards of Public Decency

Advertisements should contain nothing indecent, vulgar or repulsive which is likely, in the light of generally prevailing standards of decency and propriety, to cause grave or widespread offence.

CHAPTER - III

To Safeguard against the Indiscriminate Use of Advertising in Situations or for the Promotion of Products which are Regarded as Hazardous to Society or to Individuals to a degree or of a type which is Unacceptable to Society at Large

1. No advertisement shall be permitted which :

   (a) Tends to incite people to crime or to promote disorder and violence or intolerance.
   (b) Derides any race, caste, colour, creed or nationality.
   (c) Presents criminality as desirable or directly or indirectly encourages people—particularly children—to emulate it or conveys the modus operandi of any crime.
   (d) Adversely affects friendly relations with a foreign State.

2. Advertisements addressed to children shall not contain anything, whether in illustration or otherwise, which might result in their physical, mental or moral harm or which exploits their vulnerability. For example, no advertisement :

   (a) Shall encourage children to enter strange places or to converse with strangers in an effort to collect coupons, wrappers, labels or the like.
   (b) Should depict children leaning dangerously outside windows, over bridges or climbing dangerous cliffs and the like.
   (c) Should show children climbing or reaching dangerously to reach products or for any other purpose.
   (d) Should show children using or playing with matches or any inflammable or explosive substance; or playing with or using sharp knives, guns or mechanical or electrical appliances, the careless use of which could lead to their suffering cuts, burns, shocks or other injury.
   (e) Shall feature minors for tobacco or alcohol based products.

3. Advertisements shall not, without justifiable reason, show or refer to dangerous practices or manifest a disregard for safety or encourage negligence.
4. Advertisements should contain nothing which is in breach of the law, or omit anything which the law requires.
5. Advertisements shall not propagate products, the use of which is banned under the law.

CHAPTER - IV

To Ensure that Advertisements Observe Fairness in Competition such that the Consumer's Need to be Informed on Choices in the Market-place and the Canons of Generally Accepted Competitive Behaviour in Business are both Served.

1. Advertisements containing comparisons with other manufacturers or suppliers or with other products, including those where a competitor is named, are permissible in the interests of vigorous competition and public enlightenment, provided :
   (a) It is clear what aspects of the advertiser's product are being compared with what aspects of the competitor's product.

(b) The subject matter of comparison is not chosen in such a way as to confer an artificial advantage upon the advertiser or so as to suggest that a better bargain is offered than is truly the case.

(c) The comparisons are factual, accurate and capable of substantiation.

(d) There is no likelihood of the consumer being misled as a result of the comparison, whether about the product advertised or that with which it is compared.

(e) The advertisement does not unfairly denigrate, attack or discredit other products, advertisers or advertisements directly or by implication.

2. Advertisements shall not make unjustifiable use of the name or initials of any other firm, company or institution, nor take unfair advantage of the goodwill attached to the trade mark or symbol of another firm or its product or the goodwill acquired by its advertising campaign.

3. Advertisements shall not be so similar to other advertisements in general layout, copy, slogans, visual presentations, music or sound effects as to be likely to mislead or confuse consumers.

ANNEXURE VI

DEVELOPING TELEVISION SYSTEM FOR INDIA

Television is an ideal medium to convey information and news to broad masses of people particularly to the illiterate segment of the population, on whom such an audio-visual medium would have a profound impact.

The following questions immediately arise in developing a television system for India.

(a) Should one concentrate on providing the benefits first to urban communities and progressively go to rural areas? Direct broadcast of TV from a satellite represents the use of an advanced technology, which for the first time does not impose a penalty on account of the dispersal of the receiving units away from urban centres. The Indian economy in the next two or three decades must lean heavily on the development of rural areas. It, therefore, seems to me urgently necessary to take effective steps to enrich life in the isolated rural communities. Moreover, for continued stability and national integration, following the division of the country into linguistic administrative units, there is need to bring together different units through a common mass media of communication reaching all sections of the population, the young and the old, men and women, the literate and the illiterate, the privileged and the under-privileged. I would submit, therefore, that the answer to this question can be clearly stated. It is that we should consciously reach the most difficult and least developed areas of the country and, because they are in this state, we should reach them in a hurry.

(b) In a state of economic and social backwardness, do we need to

---

Excerpts from, Mass and Development, by Vikram Sarabhai, originally presented at a conference of the Society for International Development in New Delhi, November 1969.

deploy imaginatively the most powerful techniques at our disposal or can we get by with less effective means? In concrete terms, can radio be an alternative to television? I suggest that television has a unique contribution to make, because, it has a rare credibility and is most persuasive.

(c) Can we regard TV largely as an instrument for development, an investment rather than an overhead of society? The answer to this question depends clearly on how we use the medium and who uses it. I cannot help noting that much depends on the objectives and the assumptions of those, who create the operating system. This is because the living culture of the system is determined by the people who are associated with it. I have no quarrel with those who wish to provide entertainment through media of mass communication for society, certainly needs entertainment. But, I cannot see the same people determining policies and programming content related to education of instruction through the same medium.

(d) Recognising that Government has a number of different agencies responsible for individual fields such as information and broadcasting, education, agriculture, health, family planning, etc., how can one provide effective management of the system as a whole, along with use by the respective agencies of this powerful medium as an integral part of their promotional efforts? I would suggest that it should be possible for the other agencies to buy television time for programmes related to the discharge of their own responsibilities.

(e) Since Government has a very powerful role in promoting development, how can one prevent bureaucratisation of the system of mass communications with television? What could be the organisational framework in which programming initiative can be developed competitively amongst independent groups of innovative and imaginative producers and artists instead of through a monopolistic system, where just a few, official units produce all the programmes that are required? I would suggest that creation of a national authority, such as INTELSAT in the international scene, which merely owns, regulates and manages the mass communication system without itself taking total responsibility for software. Moreover, we should promote the development of agencies on a basis of redundancy to competitively provide software for individual clients who would buy time on the television system for promoting national objectives, which fall within subjects allocated to them. One would have to provide a feed-back system and an evaluation system to assist software development for developmental purposes.

It is quite clear that the problems of management and of software for television system to perform the role of an initiator of change and development are more formidable than the problem of hardware development. But, when we have worked through our problems and learnt through experience, we would have gained something far more precious from the standpoint of development than the television system.

ANNEXURE VII

COMMUNICATION POLICIES

The basic problem is that of linking communication facilities and activities to other national objectives or, in other words, that of integrating communication development into overall development plans. Since communication is not an autonomous, separate sector, in this domain perhaps more than in others interdependence makes it essential to develop communication policies which are not limited to information, even less to mass media—they have to take into consideration all ways and means a society needs and can utilize for its overall development purposes. We must not lose sight of the fact that communication policies go hand in hand with those fomulated in other fields, i.e. education, culture and science, and should be designed to supplement them. Communication should interrelate with these other sectors, so as to promote social, educational, scientific and other services. On the other hand, these policies should be limited to structural and material issues, and not be used to dictate content of communication or restrict expression of diverse opinions.

> A quotation from the report *What now? Another Development* (by the Dag Hammarskjöld Foundation, Uppsala, 1975) summarizes the basic new directions : "Development of every man and woman—of the whole man and woman—and not just the growth of things, which are merely means. Development geared to the satisfaction of needs beginning with the basic needs of the poor who constitute the world's majority; at the same time, development to ensure the humanization of man by the satisfaction of his needs for expression, creativity, conviviality, and for deciding his own destiny... Another development requires

---

Relevant excerpts from the Report of the International Commission for the Study of Communication Problems.

> transformation of socio-economic and political structures that have long been identified. They include such fundamental steps as agrarian reforms, urban reforms, reforms of the commercial and financial circuits, redistribution of wealth and means of production as well as the redesigning of political institutions through, inter alia, decentralization with a view to ensuring democratization of the political and economic decision-making power, promoting self-management and curbing the grip of bureaucracies. As history shows, few of these transformations can be achieved without changing the power structure itself."

It is self-evident that communication policies must also take account of demographic factors and of their consequences at different levels for development strategies. By the end of the century, it is reckoned that the world population will rise to over six billion, i.e. over two billion more than in 1975, of which the populations of the developing countries will represent over five billion. Communication policies must provide for the development of resources needed to satisfy the requirements of the various population sectors : for example the elderly, whose numbers seem certain to increase (according to UN figures, the population aged 65 to 80 and over will have roughly doubled by the year 2000, as compared with what it was in 1970), as a result of the increase in life expectancy and the drop in the birth rates; or again, in the case of the young, whose age group (generally taken to include those between 15 and 24) represents on average 7 to 10 per cent of the entire population and comprises students and young workers. Adding the number of all school-age children, aged six and over, which is increasing very considerably—above all in developing countries—it is not difficult to forecast the scale of certain needs, such as paper production for the manufacture of textbooks. These, and other such problems, are also part of communication policies which seek appropriate solutions for expansion of resources, infrastructures, facilities, equipment, etc.

With an eye to this new model of development which entails the people's involvement in the nation's affairs and which enables each citizen to affirm his or her personal and cultural ideology, the essential objective of any communications policy, particularly for developing countries, must be to provide each nation with the infrastructures in general, with telecommunications and media in particular, best suited to its needs. It is of course true that economic, industrial and technical development is an important factor in raising the living standards of peoples and nations, and must, therefore, be pursued and reinforced. But here as elsewhere, since the main consideration is people, communication between men is fundamental to the qualitative improvement of human life and human societies. The fostering and democratization of such communication may help to bring about another form of development concerned with the quality of life rather than with the variety and quantity of consumer goods alone.

While the need for national communication policies may be more or less universal, it should be noted that their formulation and content differ very widely. They do not necessarily imply rigid, centralized planning, but may simply constitute a favourable framework for the coordination of activities, allowing flexibility and a wide choice of approaches. On the other hand, what they do call for is the allocation of public resources, decisions about general structures for communication activities, elimination of internal and external imbalances, and definition of priorities, which naturally vary from one country to another.

The number of countries which frame national communication policies or which adopt general policy measures geared to the same objectives is constantly increasing. This is an essential trend and should be encouraged; however, these policies and measures should not lead to restrictions on cultural and information exchanges, but to decreasing barriers and inequalities inside and between different societies. The formulation of communication policies should : (a) serve to marshal national resources; (b) strengthen the coordination of existing or planned infrastructures; (c) facilitate rational choices with regard to means; (d) help to satisfy the needs of the most disadvantaged and to eliminate the most flagrant imbalances; (e) emphasize universal and continuing education; (f) help in strengthening cultural identity and natinal independence; (g) enable all countries and all cultures to play a more prominent role on the international scene.

Communication policies and development strategies, considered as essential means of solving the major problems of our time, should be designed first and foremost to ensure that the media of "information" become the media of "communication". Because communication presupposes access, participation and exchange, different media should be involved in the process of democratizing communication. It is here that the links between the democratization of communication and the democratization of development become apparent. For if communication policies are to be aimed at democratizing communication, and if, in addition, they must essentially be designed to be integrated into development programmes, then it is vital for those concerned to participate in the work of programming and decision-taking. There are many ways of achieving this, provided that the political will exists in the first place.

Both in the developed and developing countries, communication policies can be defined and formulated only with the collaboration of all those entities which incarnate the active forces of the countries themselves. In order to ensure that such policies, and the plans deriving from them, are duly implemented, countries must rely first and foremost upon themselves. This is a point which cannot be too strongly stressed—one which in the first instance concerns the developing countries, well aware as they are of the need to reduce their dependence in matters of information and communication. Where they exist—and even if they have to be strengthened and increased—foreign aid schemes can make only a supplementary contribution to the policy of self-development and to endogenous efforts to mobilize national resources. This policy and these efforts must naturally be pursued by the developing countries in accordance with their specific situations, needs and local realities.

ANNEXURE VIII

NATIONAL DOORDARSHAN COUNCIL

For Doordarshan to have the functional autonomy necessary for the exercise of professionalism, we recommend the following further steps :

(i) The Minister should have the benefit of advice not only from the proposed Information Board (See Chapter on Information) but additionally from a National Doordarshan Council to be formed by the Government which will include members competent, by virtue of their expertise and wide experience in the field to tender advice to the Minister on the broad social objectives, and the modes, of TV programming in the area of their knowledge and concern.

(ii) Doordarshan should receive directives not from officers of the Ministry's secretariat acting on their own but from the Minister or his deputy.

(iii) Doordarshan should be headed by a Director-General who has a proven record of excellence in any area of social communication, as well as the leadership qualities necessary for attracting and utilising creative talent in the service of the people of the country through Doordarshan.

(iv) Each Doordarshan Kendra should have a programme Advisory Council comprising members with expertise in different subjects as well as a broad social concern with problems of human resource development. The recommendations of the Kendra Advisory Council if they are unanimous or by consensus, would be binding on the Kendra unless the Minister over-rules particular recommendations as being contrary to the policy of the Government. The Kendra advisory council will be in addition to

---

Excerpts from the Report of the Working Group on Software for Doordarshan.

functional committee dealing with rural programmes, School broadcasts, etc.

We proceed to discuss the implications of some of the recommendations outlined above.

As regards the composition of the proposed National Doordarshan Council, it is recommended that its meetings should be presided over by the Minister in charge of Information & Broadcasting, or in his absence by his deputy. The members will be, from within the Government, the Director-General of Doordarshan who will be the Convenor, Secretary of the Ministry, the Financial Advisor to the Ministry, and the Chief Engineer of Doordarshan. From outside the government, members numbering six to eight would be drawn from among persons with an outstanding record of knowledge and experience in one or more of the areas of : formal and non-formal education, the art and literature, news and current affairs, conscientisation and mobilisation of women, agriculture and rural development, industry, science and technology, the organising of self-employed producers and workers in agriculture and industry, communication research and advertising; and sports.

The Council should meet at least each quarter and oftener as necessary. We see three roles for the National Doordarshan Council, as a body that reviews and guides the organisation's performance, as a guardian of Doordarshan's functional and professional autonomy, and as a counterpart of the Press Council for examining complaints of inaccuracy on bias in the reporting of news and comment on current affairs. We have discussed the need for the third role, as an Ombudsman, in the Chapter on Information.

The term of the Council could be three years. Circumstances permitting, it will be desirable in the interest of continuity, at the time of reconstitution of the Council, to have two or three of the members continue for a second term.

Had a National Doordarshan Council of the kind envisaged by us been in existence, it would have been difficult to divert Doordarshan's Non Lapsable Fund, created from its commercial advertising revenue for the purpose of improving the software, for the hardware purpose of installing low power transmitters on the eve of the Ninth Asian Games. Officialdom in the Ministry of Information & Broadcasting and in Doordarshan would be less readily plaint and more likely to function professionally and to tender objective advice to the political level of Government, if there is an institution like the proposed National Doordarshan Council.

ANNEXURE IX

EXCERPTS FROM THE NATIONAL MEDIA POLICY: A WORKING PAPER*

Objectives

The National Media Policy should lay the broad framework of the relationship of the Government with both national and international media such as Television (domestic, foreign and cable), Video, Internet, Radio, Newspaper, Film, etc. Its broad objective should be to help a citizen of the country to realise his or her potential best. The reach of print media is limited to the literate people only whereas the Electronic Media—Radio and Television—has entered the house-holds of the people all over the country. Thus, it has the viewership of all kind—adult as well as minor, illiterate as well as literate, poor as well as rich. Slightly different is the approach of film media which has also the viewership of both illiterate and literate, but its viewership is basically voluntary. Its visual impact though is much more than that of print media on both educated as well as uneducated.

Accordingly, the Sub-Committee proposes the following objectives:

Not to permit growth of monopoly in any media;

To project the developmental needs and social, cultural and economic aspirations of the people, particularly in the rural areas who constitute a bulk of our population;

To strengthen, preserve and promote our democratic traditions, culture and values, national integration and scientific temper;

To promote and strengthen sense of national integrity built on secularism, socio-cultural pluralism and linguistic diversities (unity in diversity);

---

*Submitted by the Sub-Committee of the Consultative Committee of the Ministry of Information & Broadcasting on 29 March 1996.

To facilitate greater access to information, education and entertainment in that order to all sections of the people;

To enable development in the wake of challenges thrown up by rapid technology;

To provide wider choice to the people in matters of information and entertainment;

To act as catalysts for social change;

To broadly ensure that discrimination based on gender, religion, caste, language, etc. is not directly or indirectly practiced or promoted and portrayal of any section of the society is not done in a derogatory manner.

Nature of Media Policy

As regards the question as to whether there should be a single media policy covering all media or separate for each of them, we need to look at the present status of various media. As far as the print media is concerned, it is in the private hands and Government has no direct role in its functioning. It is also pertinent to note that the reach of print media is only to the literate people and that too in urban areas in particular. There is Press Council of India to oversee the activities of the print media so that it functions within the given parameters laid down in the various enactments and the Constitution of India. Also, the Sub-Committee notes that the Press, over a period of time, jealously guards its freedom and is the most popular vehicle for dissent and pluralism in views.

Regarding film media, it is also largely in private hands and Government's control is only about certifying the cinematographic films which are screened for the public exhibition. The development of theatres to facilitate the proper exhibition of films to all categories of the people is also one of the aspects looked into by the Government. The reach of the film media is to both literate as well as illiterate, the same as electronic media, but the decision to see a film is a voluntary act as it requires money and time on the part of the viewers.

As stated above, electronic media has a global reach. It reaches not only within the boundaries of the country but by modern technology and innovation of satellite, it can reach to any remotest area of the world subject to the uplinking facilities. At present, the electronic media is controlled by the Government but that is applicable only in case of country based programmes whereas there is no control on the programmes which are beamed through satellite by foreign lands in the country.

In the light of the above, it may appear that various media are so divergent that a single media policy may be difficult. The Sub-Committee had considered this question in detail and felt that the objectives chosen are general in nature and can be applicable for all the media. Therefore, it recommends that at macro-level, there should be a single media policy encompassing all the three media—print, film and electronic, but at operational level, each media should have its own detailed guidelines according to its reach, viewership/listeners/readership as the case may be.

Summary of Recommendations

Electronic Media

The broadcasting should observe a greater degree of responsibility and sensitivity to Indian culture and ethos and cater to the developmental requirement of the country. It should achieve an Indian personality in telecasting/broadcasting.

There should be a regulatory body to oversee both public and private telecasting/broadcasting. In this connection, the Sub-Committee noted that the provisions of the Prasar Bharati Act, which was unanimously passed by Parliament in 1990 should be kept in mind while framing the regulatory mechanism which should be an independent autonomous authority. The Sub-Committee is of confirmed opinion that no recourse should be taken by the Government to dilute the provision of the Prasar Bharati Act, 1990. This regulatory body may be set up to ensure adherence to the programmes/advertisement codes and other stipulations. This body or similar independent body may also develop an effective mechanism for public grievance redressal as well as implementation of its recommendations in respect of such grievances.

Adequate care should be taken to enable the setting up of non-commercial broadcasting stations to be run by universities, educational institutions, panchayats/local bodies, State Governments, etc.

The Sub-Committee recognises that for public broadcasting, adequate funding in the form of state support is necessary. The content of programmes or software is often dictated by the funding and therefore the Sub-Committee strongly recommends that this aspect should receive the attention of the government and an institutional system be worked out.

The national broadcasters—Akashvani and Doordarshan—should bear the responsibility to offer a high quality public service broadcasting that informs, educates and entertains the people and also provide coverage to national events like the Republic Day Parade. Taking into account the reach of the national broadcasters, primacy and exclusive responsibility should be provided to them in the matter of coverage of national events like Republic Day Parade, Independence Day, the President's Address to both the Houses of Parliament, etc.

The rights/obligations and exclusivity of the national broadcasters should be codified through law.

Whereas the broad policy approach should be the same for radio and television, minor variations/differences can be made in view of the difference in reach and impact of the two media. Programme/advertisement codes should be similar, if not, same. The viewer/listener interest should be kept in mind while spacing the advertisements. A new production style, which is people-oriented should be developed.

In tune with the policy framework suggested here, the Indian private sector/State Government/NGOs/Local Self Government should be allowed to enter the field of broadcasting/telecasting.

Appropriate provisions must be made to ensure that the control of private broadcasting does not fall in the hands of companies having major stake in the print medium or vice-versa. Cross-media ownership restrictions must, therefore, be considered.

Direct or indirect foreign equity participation in companies entering the field of private broadcasting should not be permitted.

Access on the private channel should be available to the common man through appropriate provisions in the law.

In view of the Supreme Court's Judgement on airwaves, an independent authority must be set up to control and regulate the use of airwaves. The Sub-Committee felt that the integrity of the Indian Skies is as important as her territorial integrity. This regulatory authority must be set up through a law enacted by the Parliament at the earliest. This Body can combine the functions of the regulatory body mentioned in para 6.4.1.2 or can be a separate body exclusively for controlling the sky waves under the regulatory body mentioned in para 6.4.1.2.

The apex regulatory body should be an independent autonomous public authority representative of all sections and interests in the society and should control and regulate the use of air waves in the interests of the public and to prevent invasion of their rights.

The foreign satellite channels must also be brought within the ambit of the said regulatory body in order to make them amenable to the Indian laws.

The Sub-Committee felt that in the case of skywaves, efforts should be made to develop an international convention to forge multilateral/

agreements with countries especially in regard to software.

The Sub-Committee noted that it will be difficult to pre-censor programmes aired on television in view of vast structure such a step would call for. By bringing in the private broadcasting/foreign channels within the purview of the Indian legal system, much of laissez-faire that exists can be curbed.

The Sub-Committee felt that the present programming in electronic media, especially television, needs to be more decentralised to meet the regional/local aspirations. In this connection, the Verghese Committee recommendations regarding decentralised programming, programme autonomy and constitution of five zones for this purpose (viz. South, West, Central, Eastern and North) should be considered by the Government.

Care should be taken that no monopoly is developed by the private broadcasters, by restructuring the number of channels, especially 'several interest' channels owned by them.

Film Media

The Sub-Committee agrees with the broad objectives of national film policy set out by the Working Group on National Film Policy, vide para 7.6.2 above and we reiterate the same. As a formal declaration of the national film policy would be useful, the Sub-Committee recommends that the Government should formalise the same as early as possible.

Since the Estimates Committee and the Standing Committee have examined in detail the working of the CBFC as mentioned above, we have nothing further to add except to reiterate their recommendations. These recommendations are discussed elsewhere (vide Annexure-VII and paras 7.9.5 and 7.9.6). The Sub-Committee wishes to add that Government should amend the guidelines for certification of films to curb the distortion of image of eminent leaders in films.

The production of good short films, both by Films Division and independent producers, needs to be actively encouraged. The Films Division should make efforts to improve the quality of its documentaries and make them more interesting. The Sub-Committee recommends that Government should encourage the growth of Indian documentary film movement. The Sub-Committee suggests in this regard that the Films Division should farm out more and more films to independent producers on its panel. Further, Doordarshan should commission production of documentaries through the Films Division and other agencies.

It has been stated that it would be very difficult to find sponsors for telecasting documentaries on Doordarshan. The Sub-Committee recommends that the Doordarshan should allot time-slots for at least half-an-hour every day on prime time for documentaries, even if there are no sponsors.

The Sub-Committee also recommends that the feasibility of showing documentary films in various educational institutions, schools, colleges and universities should be examined. The Ministry of Human Resources Development should consider the allocation of funds for the purpose.

With a view to encourage children's films, the Sub-Committee recommends that more infrastructural facilities should be developed for production of animation films.

The Sub-Committee also recommends that more avenues for exhibition of children's films in each district of the country should be identified.

During meetings, representatives of the film industry pointed out that though Government called for recommendations from the Film Federation of India for the Dadasaheb Phalke Award, it did not normally accept their recommendation. The Sub-Committee is informed that Government gets recommendations from all quarters including film industry and the best person is selected at the highest level in the Ministry for the Award. To give more credibility to the Government's decision, the Sub-Committee would recommend that a small Committee consisting of eminent persons including those from Film World should be appointed by Government to consider all names received and recommend the name of the person who should be honoured with the Dadasaheb Phalke Award.

The National Film Awards were instituted in 1953 to provide for a special impetus to regional cinema and to encourage the production of films of aesthetic excellence and social relevance. The Sub-Committee also recommends that the award winning films should be screened at various State capitals and other large towns so that the people in the regional centres may get an opportunity to see them. The Central Government should provide funds to the State Governments to organise such festivals of award-winning films.

A number of witnesses before the Sub-Committee represented for the full implementation of the recommendations of the High Powered Committee (1990). The Sub-Committee would suggest that the matter should be taken up with the various State Governments/Union Territory Administrations again.

The Sub-Committee recommends that the State Governments/ Union Territory Administrations should be persuaded to rationalise the rates of Entertainment Tax to help the film industry.

During discussions some of the film industry representatives represented to the Sub-Committee that in view of high cost of imported raw stock, the customs countervailing duty may be reduced if not abolished. The Sub-Committee recommends that the countervailing duty on raw stock may be abolished in view of the fact that there are no facilities to manufacture the raw stock in the country.

Some of the witnesses before the Sub-Committee expressed concern about the shortage of theatres as well as the closure of cinema houses due to the advent of television and video. To overcome the shortage of exhibition facilities, the Sub-Committee suggests that wherever cinema theatres are being converted into commercial complexes, the local authorities should ensure that in the complex coming up at the site at least one mini theatre is provided in the complex. The Sub-Committee would also recommend that more multiplex theatrical complexes should be encouraged.

The Sub-Committee recommends that the National Film Development Corporation and other agencies should encourage construction of theatres with 400 to 500 capacity instead of very large theatres.

During meetings the representatives of the cine workers pleaded for the declaration of the film industry as an "Industry" so that the workers of the industry are not exploited by the producers. The Sub-Committee feels that introduction of labour welfare measures to film industry workers will go a long way in improving their conditions. The Sub-Committee, therefore, recommends that the film industry may be declared as an industry not only for the purpose of institutional finance but also for application of labour legislation relating to welfare of labour.

The National Film Archive of India is charged with the responsibility of preservation of cinema. There have been press reports about the damage and loss of important films. The Sub-Committee suggests that the Archive should take immediate steps to acquire all film classics and preserve them properly for posterity.

The Sub-Committee also suggests that the National Film Archive of India should take over the old documentaries from the Films Division for restoration and preservation.

Now-a-days film appreciation courses have been started in various universities and new film societies are coming up. However, Government gives only Rs. 3 lakhs per year to the Federation of Film Societies of India for its activities. This is awfully inadequate. The Sub-Committee recommends that Government should encourage film society movement by giving all facilities including finance. The grant-in-aid to the Federation of Film Societies of India should be augmented suitably.

Some of the witnesses informed the Sub-Committee that Akashvani's royalty rates for film songs which broadcast is Rs. 2 per song and was fixed a long time ago. Considering the time lapse and increase in cost of picturising film songs, the Sub-Committee recommends that this should be suitably revised upwards by Akashvani.

Print Media

With respect to the suggestions regarding evolving a code of conduct for the journalists and for vesting the Press Council of India with more powers, the Sub-Committee felt that the matter may be left to the Press Council for suitable decisions. However, the Press Council should consider arming itself with adequate powers to deal with habitual offences with respect to communalism, threats to national security and other undesirable activities.

The language Press and the small and medium newspapers should continue to grow. Therefore, the Sub-Committee recommends that the Government must endeavour to create a suitable environment by helping in the modernisation of these sections of the Press.

Though the financial viability of a newspaper depends to a larger extent on the advertisement revenue which it is able to attract, Government's advertising policy and rate structure should be rational and uniform, evolved with a view to eliminate the possible use of advertisements as a lever to influence the press and thereby affecting its freedom.

Even though the import of newsprint has been put under OGL, there is a need for a nodal agency to import newsprint on behalf of small and medium newspapers as they do not have the necessary infrastructure and the bargaining power for such imports.

The training requirements of the journalists is yet another aspect which needs immediate attention. The press over the years has to become increasingly professional in nature. With a view to ensure that the press as a whole is capable of reporting and explaining and interpreting in their proper perspective various developments taking place, it is imperative that additional facilities are created to enable journalists to have a broad educational preparation and specific training in journalism.

Indian news agencies have not been able to operate effectively in the sphere of dissemination of national news abroad, and the gathering of foreign news for dissemination within the country. Foreign news agencies still dominate international news sections in leading newspapers. It should be the endeavour of the Government to permit and strengthen the news agencies to become self-sufficient in these spheres. In this connection, renewed efforts should be made in revitalising the efforts taken in the wake of Non-Aligned Conference, 1976 which lead to the establishment of Newspool for exchange of news among the third world countries.

To strengthen the Indian news agencies, the Sub-Committee recommends that corporatisation of these news agencies with adequate equity base, as was suggested by the First Press Commission, should be seriously considered.

Freedom of the editors, and editorial contents, insulated from the business and other interests of the owners, should be ensured through a proper institutional mechanism or guidelines to be evolved by the Press themselves or by the Press Council of India. The issue of diversion of funds from the newspaper industry to other industries may be examined.

The Sub-Committee feels that towards professionalisation of the print media, adequate institutional finance should be made available to the journalists, etc. through cooperatives on easy terms.

CONTRIBUTORS

1. **A. Sengupta**, Joint Secretary, Indian Space Research Organization, Bangalore.
2. **Abdur Rahim**, Professor, Department of Communication and Journalism, Osmania University, Hyderabad.
3. **C. Jayanthi**, Staff Reporter, *The Pioneer*, New Delhi.
4. **Jag Mohan**, Executive Secretary, Namedia Foundation, New Delhi.
5. **M. R. Dua**, Professor & Head, Department of Journalism, Indian Institute of Mass Communication, New Delhi.
6. **Nandini Prasad**, Programme Adviser, Women and Development, Royal Netherlands Embassy, New Delhi.
7. **Prem Kumar**, Veteran Journalist and Former Editor, *Indian Express*, Chandigarh.
8. **Rajeshwar Dyal**, Media Adviser, Friedrich Ebert Stiftung, New Delhi.
9. **Sharita Rai**, Special Correspondent, *Indian Express*, Bangalore.
10. **Sunil Misra**, Director (Retd.), Audience Research, All India Radio, New Delhi.
11. **Sunil Saxena**, Dean, Asian College of Journalism, Bangalore.
12. **V. S. Gupta,** Professor, Directorate of Publications, Haryana Agricultural University, Hisar.
13. **Vijayluxmi Bose**, Media Researcher, Department of Journalism and Mass Communication, Jamia Milia Islamia University, New Delhi.
14. **Vir Bala Aggarwal**, Assistant Professor, Department of Journalism and Mass Communication, Himachal Pradesh University, Shimla.

BIBLIOGRAPHY

Agnihotri, V. K. (1995) (ed.). *Public Policy, Analysis and Design*. New Delhi : Concept Publishing Company.

Akash Bharati : National Broadcast Trust, Vol. I. (1978). Report of the Working Group on Autonomy for Akashvani and Doordarshan, New Delhi : Ministry of Information and Broadcasting.

An Indian Personality for T.V., Vol. I. (1985). Report of the Working Group on Software for Doordarshan, New Delhi : Publications Division.

Bhargava, G. S. (ed.) (1991). *Government Media—Autonomy and After*. New Delhi : Concept Publishing Company.

Chawla, N. L. (1982). Communication Policy in India—Software Production and Distribution. *Communicator,* XVII (I) : 2-6, 10.

Friedrich Ebert Stiftung, Bonn. (1984). New Communication Technologies and their Impact on Western Industrialized Countries. Communication Manual.

Goonasekera, Anura. (1993). Media Technology and Social Imperatives. An Examination of Communication Policies in Selected Asian Countries. *Media Asia*, 20 (4) : 194-204.

Gupta, V. S. (1981). Communication Planning—A plea for appropriate communication. *Media Asia* 8 (3) : 156-161.

Gupta, V. S. (1995). *Third Revolution in Indian Perspective—Contemporary Issues and Themes in Communication*. New Delhi : Concept Publishing Company.

Gupta. V. S. and Vir Bala Aggarwal (1996). *Media Policy and Nation Building—Select Issues and Themes.* New Delhi: Concept Publishing Company.

Joshi, P. C. (1986). *Communication and Nation Building : Perspective and Policy*. Sardar Patel Memorial Lectures (1995), New Delhi: Publications Division.

Khan, Rahat Nabi (1987). The Third Industrial Revolution : An Economic Overview. *Impact of Science on Society,* 146: 115-122, UNESCO.

Lee, John A. R. (1976). *Towards Realistic Communication Policies.* Recent Trends and Ideas Compiled and Analysed. UNESCO.

Luthra, H. R. (1986). *Indian Broadcasting.* New Delhi : Publications Division, Ministry of Information and Broadcasting, Govt. of India.

Masani, Mehra (1976). *Broadcasting and the People.* New Delhi : National Book Trust.

Mass Media in India (1993). New Delhi : Publications Division, Government of India.

Menon, Narayana (1976). *The Communication Revolution.* New Delhi: National Book Trust, p. 86.

Michael Kunczik (1991). *Communication and Social Change.* Friedrich Ebert-Stiftung, Bonn.

Ministry of Information and Broadcasting (1994-95). *Annual Report.* New Delhi : Publications Division, Govt. of India.

Ministry of Information and Broadcasting (1994-95). *Mass Media in India.* New Delhi : Publications Division, Govt. of India.

National Media Policy—A Working Paper (March 1996). Submitted by the Sub-Committee of the Consultative Committee of the Ministry of Information and Broadcasting, New Delhi.

Mowlana, Hamid and Laurie, Wilson J. (1988). *Communication Technology and Development.* Reports and Papers on Mass Communication No. 101. UNESCO.

National Media Policy (1995). *A Discussion Paper.* New Delhi : Ministry of Information and Broadcasting.

Sawant, B. P., Mohan, S. and Reddy, B. P. Jeevan (1995). Supreme Court Judgement in Civil Appeals Nos. 1429-30 : Secretary, Ministry of Information and Broadcasting vs Cricket Association of Bengal.

Sayani, Ameen (1993). National and Transnational Censorship—Guidelines and Advertising Codes for Radio and Television. Paper presented at AMIC Seminar on the Legal and Regulatory Aspects of Satellite Broadcasting, New Delhi, 22-23 October.

Singhal, Arvind and Rogers, Everett, M. (1989). *India's Information Revolution.* New Delhi : Sage.

Teheranian Majid, Farhad Hakimzadeh and Marcello L. Vidale (eds.) (1977). *Communications Policy for National Development—A Comparative Perspective*. London. Routledge & Kegan, Paul.

Thomas, P. N. (1993). Information and Change in India—Cultural Politics in a Post-modern Era. *Asian Journal of Communication*. 3(1) : 64-83.

Tiwari, I. P. (1987). *Communication, Technology and Development*. New Delhi : Publications Division.

UNESCO (1982). *Many Voices, One World*. The International Commission on the Study of Communication Problems. University Grants Commission—Countrywide Classroom—A Window on the World.

Venkateswaran, K. S. (1993). *Mass Media, Laws and Regulations in India*. AMIC.

Wang, Georgette (1991). Information Society in their Mind : A Survey of College Students in Seven Nations. *Asian Journal of Communication* 1(2): 1-18.

Yadava, J. S. (1994). Communication and Development—The Indian Experience. In : *Media and Development*, Dua, M. R. and Gupta, V. S. (eds.). New Delhi : Har-Anand Publications.

INDEX